GENEVIEVE TAYLOR

SCORCHED

The ultimate guide to barbecuing fish

Photography by Jason Ingram

Hardie Grant

QUADRILLE

INTRODUCTION

Welcome to *SCORCHED*, the third in a trilogy of barbecue books that started with *CHARRED*, on vegetables, and *SEARED*, on meat. These three words are essentially identical in meaning but it felt particularly right for this, my guide to seafood over fire, where the cooking mantra is always 'hot and fast, hot and fast'. On repeat. Whereas I would happily slow-cook meat for 12 hours or more, fish cooking times are always measured in minutes.

Here the description 'seafood' encompasses all fish, mostly sea-dwelling ones – with the exception of trout – but also the shellfish, cephalopods and crustaceans we eat. It therefore covers a broad spectrum of water dwellers that, for the most part, excluding the farmed species, are as natural and free-range a thing as you could ever hope to eat. These are healthy proteins, full of vitamins, minerals and unsaturated fats and they taste amazing, at their best, when cooked over fire. They also have something of a reputation for being hard to cook – partly deserved, it's true – but I am here to hold your hand and give you the knowledge you need to turn that idea on its head.

I'm not sure there is an aroma more deliciously evocative of sunshine, holidays and past adventures than the smell of seafood cooking over fire. It just takes me back to good times and it's no coincidence that within these pages there is a lot of inspiration from the Med, like Grilled gurnard with peperonata (page 62), Real taramasalata (page 152) and Monkfish and chard paella (page 248). Other further-flung parts of the world I've been lucky enough to visit are explored, too, with the Bream with nam jim sauce and coconut rice (page 56), Cuttlefish satay with sambal kecap and grilled pak choi (page 211), Lemongrass and coconut mussels (page 216) and Sri Lankan crab curry (page 253) showcasing some of my favourite food from my favourite places.

Fire is the original cooking tool, and with two-thirds of the planet covered in oceans it should come as no surprise that the whole globe has a history of cooking fish over fire.

I'm guessing you are reading this book because you like eating seafood, so I hope to give you more confidence and many ideas with what to do with it.

Happy cooking!

@GenevieveEats

The island nation paradox

But here's a thing: 80 per cent of fish caught by British fishermen is exported. Conversely, about the same proportion of fish sold in supermarkets is imported from non-UK waters. Given that many of us now believe that eating locally is better for us, there's not much sense in that, right?

For an island nation, the British seem to be a bit scared about cooking fish, but it's far from clear whether that's the look or feel or smell of it when we cook it, or the fact that it is an expensive protein that is more delicate and fragile than meat. Do we fear failure? Many people are also put off by the head and tail and bone thing but if that includes you, I can reassure you that there's plenty within these pages that doesn't begin with a whole fish. You could also argue that by taking the cooking outside we are dealing neatly with any smelly kitchen issues, but I firmly believe the end result just tastes better when cooked outside.

Geographical scope of this book

As a European author, this book mainly features the seafood of the North Atlantic – a huge area of ocean stretching from the Arctic circle in the north to the equator at its southern extreme. Readers in the United States will have access to very many of these species as we share common ocean borders, but will also have access to fish from the Pacific Ocean. Readers in Australia and New Zealand will have access to species from the Pacific, Indian and Southern Oceans, while those in South Africa get the Southern Atlantic, the Southern Pacific and Southern Oceans.

The reality of the matter is this: **almost any fish can be paired with any sauce** ... and while some cooking methods are more suitable than others for particular types of fish, there is much bend and flex here. I don't feel like any of these recipes are 'do or die', set in stone – I'm just not that kind of cook. My natural, untamed instinct is 'toss it in and see what happens' and I encourage you to swap in this or that and adapt at your will. Where a recipe is especially

suited to an alternative seafood, I have pointed you in that direction, but being flexible with the ingredients we choose to cook is a critical way we can support sustainability, so perhaps the best way is to buy the fish first and then pick the recipe you fancy.

While I encourage you to tinker with my recipes, I do, however, consider good fuel a non-negotiable, so I steer you firmly to page 12 for that chat.

How to use this book

The temptation with a brand-new cookbook is to slide quickly through these pages to get to the recipes and their beautiful accompanying images, and while I hope I've done you proud here and that you will want to cook them all, I would urge a good read of these introductory pages. This bit at the beginning is where it hopefully all falls into place: the whys and wherefores of fire cooking, the geeky science stuff about both the fish and the fire – this is the information that will help us all learn to be better fire cooks.

Throughout the book you will encounter a liberal scattering of 'refer back to page X' or 'see page X for more detail' – not everywhere but in places where I thought a reminder was most useful. I hope this repetition is neither tedious nor annoying, but rather a reminder of the important and useful stuff within. Of course, once you have read and absorbed the information, it will become second nature. With all fire cooking the best way to learn and get better is to practise, practise, practise, and with each cook you will learn something new and gain confidence.

What is 'GOOD FISH'?

Just as with meat, the sourcing of seafood – where and how we buy it – has become an important part of the way I shop, so the idea of defining 'good' fish is an important one for me to delve into. As a biologist by training, with a background in marine biology, I couldn't write this book without touching on the ecology of the oceans and the science behind the fish and the fire I am cooking it over. I hope you find it as interesting as I do, and that it gives you a better understanding of how to buy and cook seafood.

Navigating a sustainable line through buying fish can be hard, certainly a lot harder than it is for livestock farming, where the differences between 'good', 'less good' and downright 'bad' practice are mostly pretty clear cut.

In theory, eating fish could and should be seen as a responsible choice. Certainly from a carbon-footprint perspective, I'm not sure there is a better source of high-quality protein. Wild fish need no feeding, no fertilizers, antibiotics or other chemical inputs. Although fuel and emissions from engines are a factor, a single boat can land many thousands of fish, making each individual fish very low impact indeed. With two-thirds of the planet made up of oceans, it's no wonder that fish is a major protein source globally. However, we have sadly neglected our responsibilities in this area and we do need to conserve this precious resource.

Fishing methods matter

Fish are caught in different ways depending on the types of equipment used and the species that are being fished. Different nets and equipment fish at various levels, some dredging along the seabed while others fish nearer the surface with nets or hooks and lines. The impact of the various methods depends on a huge number of variables, including frequency of use, localized populations, location and regulation, as well as the technique itself.

Some methods are less destructive than others and that relates to several factors.

- Impact on habitats and environment, especially the disturbance of the sea bed.
- Avoidance of bycatch, including both fish and other sea creatures.
- Leaving enough fish to maintain a healthy population.
- Being highly selective of abundant species.
- Avoiding an undersized catch.

As seems to be the way with fishing, the picture is constantly evolving, so head to https://www.msc.org for a concise and up-to-date guide to the main commercial fishing methods and their environmental impact.

The big five

Sustainability with seafood is clearly linked to diversity. The vast majority of the fish we buy in the UK falls into the 'big five' species: **salmon**, **cod**, **haddock**, **prawns** and **tuna**. These are certainly delicious to eat, but one simple way we could buy more responsibly is to branch out, try something new, explore species that are seasonally and locally abundant, eat fish that have been caught as 'bycatch'. The picture with fish is as fluid and moveable as they are and the story is localized and changeable. Take cod, which a few years ago was classed as in critical decline. Now, in Cornwall, cod stocks are really rather healthy, whereas the pollock we were all encouraged to eat more of is now not as prolific as it once was.

In an age where we have come to expect to be able to buy everything we fancy all year round – strawberries at Christmas? – I think it has become less obvious that fish are highly seasonal creatures, so at certain times of the year certain fish will be unavailable, full stop. We therefore need to be flexible in our approach. Once again, **'buy the fish, then choose the recipe'** is a useful place to begin.

The issues are certainly complex and, as fish know no borders, fishing is very much a global geopolitical problem. As a rule, the slower growing a species is, the more vulnerable it is to overfishing, whereas seafood that reaches adulthood quicker and breeds faster is more resilient because stocks are more rapidly replenished.

As a consumer who just wants to eat something good for dinner, the arguments can be hard to navigate, but we can arm ourselves with the current facts in order to make as responsible a choice as possible. Luckily there are great resources to help you check the latest views on the sustainability of a particular species. A good start is to buy fish with a Marine Stewardship Council (MSC) certification for wild-caught species or an Aquaculture Stewardship Council (ASC) for farmed species. These organizations certify that the fish we eat come with certain standards for sustainability and they are heavily involved in the science of good fishing practice. Heading online and checking out the Marine Conservation Society's Good Fish Guide and the Cornwall Good Seafood Guide is another great starting point. Head to page 266 for a list of useful resources.

As usual with important issues, however, the picture is not always as clear cut as we might hope. Here are two examples of things that can muddy the waters.

The bycatch issue

Bycatch is the term coined for seafood caught that is not part of the fishing plan or the boat's quota. Fish are free-flowing creatures, moving around, shoaling, congregating, travelling about their business as they choose. So, unlike a flock of sheep fenced in a field, they are genuinely free range and it is inevitable that during the fishing process some species end up caught that are not required. The chances are minimized as much as possible – using often very sophisticated ultrasonic technology as well as adjusting mesh sizes of the nets – but it still happens. It's a complex issue, like so much to do with commercial fishing, but I believe there is a very strong argument indeed for saying if it has been caught, we should eat it. Bycatch discarded back into the sea invariably won't survive and just becomes a rather gross example of food waste.

Local seasonal abundance

The other complicating issue is one of local seasonal abundance that conflicts with the wider picture. To take one example, the thornback ray is listed as a 'fish to avoid' by the Marine Conservation Guide and the Cornwall Good Seafood Guide but I know from many local sources they can be found in huge numbers in certain places at certain times of the year. Where species are found in unusual numbers, they can be damaging to the overall ecosystem as they throw it out of balance, so taking them out of the equation at such a point is a good thing.

Cuttlefish are another case in point. Off the south coast of Devon and Dorset, in the UK, they are dubbed 'black gold', because of their ink, and the fact is, cuttlefish is so abundant during the spawning season that the local fishing industry makes a substantial portion of their year's profits from the species. Most of these cuttles are exported to mainland Europe, but if you see them in UK fishmongers, they are a bit of a bargain compared to squid and just as tasty, so snap them up and try some of my cuttle recipes (pages 198–243).

The case for trout over salmon

I am a big advocate of using trout as a more responsible alternative to salmon. It's something I've come to feel so strongly about that you won't find a single salmon recipe in this book. In terms of how they cook and taste, trout is remarkably similar to salmon and I consider them to be interchangeable. Head to page 266 for some excellent trout suppliers.

So what's the problem with salmon?

A cookbook is not the place for a lengthy discussion on the good and bad aspects of the salmon farming industry but there is a vast quantity of research to be found online if you are interested in the scale of the problem. In a couple of lines, the pros are largely economic gains and the cons are gross levels of environmental destruction with fish intensively stocked in open water pens, leading to huge problems of overcrowding, disease and considerable waste pollution of the surrounding seas. Pesticides and antibiotics are very heavily relied on, which has massive knock-on effects to the wildlife all around. Not a great picture.

And why is freshwater trout better?

The Marine Conservation Society rates freshwater trout as a 'good choice' fish and a more sustainable option than sea-farmed salmon. Trout are very efficient converters of food into body mass, so they eat less, basically, and therefore produce less waste. They are farmed in freshwater pens segregated from the main watercourse and the water is filtered of waste before it is returned clean to the river.

As is usual, the picture is evolving and as better salmon farming practices come into play, they may make a return to my table, but for now it's trout all the way.

What is 'GOOD FUEL'?

I can't overestimate the importance of using the best-quality fuel on your barbecue. I consider it to be the single most important 'ingredient' in fire cooking.

Those of you who've met me at Bristol Fire School, seen me talk at festivals or read one of my rants on social media know how important using good fuel is to me. My own personal line in the sand is that I won't burn anything that's not British. While we don't often have much control about where we buy our electricity or gas, we do have absolute control when it comes to the charcoal we cook on and we can decide to buy better. I buy all my fuel online (from Whittle and Flame; the best charcoal I ever set fire to) and it is delivered overnight via a courier. So, a little more effort than grabbing a bag of the rubbish stuff from my local supermarket but in reality not that much more time-consuming.

Good charcoal is a very pure product made from wood baked at highly specific temperatures to burn off everything than isn't carbon. It's an inert substance that has no taste, smell, smoke or flavour. If you open a bag of charcoal and it smells of something, anything more than zero, it won't be pure and I would be rather happy if you didn't burn it. Sadly, most charcoal we use comes from the tropics, is badly, unethically and sometimes illegally harvested and very often contains a lot chemicals, both to stop it catching fire during the journey to us and also then, when it gets to our shores, accelerant chemicals to help us light it quickly. Simply put, when charcoal smells, this is why.

That thing we think we know about charcoal – that it should be white and ashy before we can cook on it? This is necessary only to burn off the chemicals before it is palatable and/or safe to cook on. With good charcoal, you can light and get cooking almost straight away. That said, in my vast experiments with fish cookery for this book, the kind of heat you need to cook fish is more of a burnt-down fire than a newly lit one. Head to page 28 for that story.

By investing in quality, pure lump charcoal we are also doing a positive job of supporting woodland management because somebody is earning a living from working in the wood. Managing forests properly is critical to increasing their biodiversity, allowing wildflowers, insects, birds and mammals to thrive. So please do think about where your charcoal comes from and know that you can feel good about burning the good stuff. Yes, it costs more, but if you use it carefully, as I show you, it will last longer, and besides, it's very much a price worth paying.

For those readers all over the world (why, hello!) my best advice is to hop online and search for sustainable local charcoal. It's the best place to start.

BUYING AND STORING FISH

Having established some principles, let's get back to the nitty-gritty of the subject and look at making sure we have the very best ingredients to cook with.

How and where to buy good fish

One way we can all shop more sustainably, with fish or any other food, is to think about how we can shorten the supply chain. In a simplified example, say a massive chain supermarket places an order for enough cod fillets to supply all its branches nationwide. That cod will be purchased via middlemen (brokers or merchants) off the big commercial boats fishing for vast quantities of cod around the waters of the North Atlantic. That cod needs processing, a job that's highly centralized, and very often done abroad – one the biggest fish-processing nations supplying UK supermarkets, for example, is China. So the cod you bought that was labelled as a 'British' fished product has very likely travelled half way round the world and back before you get to cook it. The more links we can remove from these huge, complex supply chains, the more sustainable the fish we buy will be. This means, where we can, prioritizing local produce, small businesses and buying directly from the producers.

Obviously in a perfect world we would love to skip off to the harbour and buy straight off the boat that caught the fish we eat, but if you don't live next to, or even remotely near, the sea (I wish!), then what do you do?

Buying seafood from small 'day boats' is always going to a more responsible choice. They fish on a smaller, non-industrialized scale, can't take as much in terms of volume and they have to fish very selectively so bycatch is less. The fish will no doubt be fresher too. As the name suggests, they go out and come back within a day, unlike the massive commercial boats which can be at sea for weeks, storing their vast fish catches on ice for longer than is probably ideal.

So we have two options here. Find a fishmonger local to you who is happy to talk about the traceability of their produce and support their business, or find an online fishmonger, of which there are many great ones. I have a great local fishmonger, Sam at Bristol Fish, who is always happy for me to quiz him and I buy most of my fish from him. I also buy from several specialist online fishmongers, and even direct from the boat, or fish farms in the case of trout. If the COVID lockdowns had one big positive in the UK, it gave us confidence that buying fresh produce online is actually a very viable option and it's now something I do often. It's a brilliant way to cut out some links in the supply chain that will make your food more sustainable (see page 8 on 'good fish' and pages 266–269 for suppliers).

How to tell freshness

Fish deteriorates quickly, and while many high-end chefs are experimenting with 'dry ageing' fish, in a domestic situation, fresh is always going to win taste-wise. Here are the top four things to look out for when buying fish. Obviously if you are buying online – and it's a great way to buy fish – then you need to trust that the fishmonger has done the choosing for you. If fish arrives and it is not adequate, you need to let them know pronto, then take your business elsewhere.

Eyes: Should be bright and shiny with black pupils and a convex (rounded out), slightly bulging shape.

Gills: Should be bright red, indicating a good supply of oxygen. As the fish ages post death, the gills lose brightness as the oxygen depletes, so gills that aren't bright indicate the fish is not as fresh as it could be.

Smell: Fresh fish shouldn't smell fishy, it should smell fresh and 'ocean-y'. Overly fishy smells indicate the production of ammonia derivatives as enzymes break down the flesh.

Mucus: The fish's body should be firm and shiny but the mucus that creates that shine should not smell unpleasant. It does an important job by protecting the fish from pathogens, and a fresher fish will be good and slimy.

Why does fish 'go off' quicker than meat?

With any food item that deteriorates quickly, correct storage is especially important.

Fish are full of highly unsaturated fats that remain liquid in the cold aquatic environment, so the fish can flex and swim, and it's this unsaturated nature that makes fish a super-healthy protein. It's perhaps helpful to compare butter to olive oil – the former being solid and arguably not very good for us, the latter fluid and a more healthy option.

It also makes fish more perishable than meat as these fats are less stable on exposure to oxygen, breaking down quicker in the air. Also, the bacteria naturally within the fish, and the enzymes needed for the fish's bodily function, both operate efficiently at much lower temperatures. This means they are active even at fridge temperatures, spoiling the fish quicker. The warm-blooded mammals and birds we eat have enzymes that function at higher temperatures, some 40°C (104°F) or so, meaning that while a fridge is positively chilly for a piece of beef (therefore preserving it), it is actually not that chilly at all for a piece of fish (so it deteriorates quicker). In short, you need to keep your fish as cold as possible before you cook it and use it as quickly as you can.

How to store in the fridge

I have a dedicated raw meat and fish drawer at the bottom of my fridge where it is colder. Once I have bought fish, it is either frozen immediately or, if I plan to eat it within a day, placed unwrapped on trays with racks over (page 23) to dry out the skin (so important to help with the sticking problem, see page 26). Storing fish in a drier environment also helps it stay fresh, while storing in a wet environment – so in a bag where it is surrounded by water and its own juices – will promote deterioration.

Occasionally people question the fact the fish is uncovered, as in 'isn't that risky from a health and safety point of view?' but as long as the fish is on a tray that can catch any drips and it is not overhanging or touching anything else, it is just fine. Potential pathogens or bacteria cannot leap through the air to spoil other foods so containment is key.

Freezing fish

As I mentioned, the colder the fish is stored, the less quickly the enzymes and bacteria can spoil it, so 'supercooling' by freezing is a great way to store fish, even if only for a few days. If I buy fish online and can't cook and eat it within a day, it will head into my freezer. Well wrapped to prevent freezer burn, white fish will last for up to six months in a deep freeze. Oily fish – trout, mackerel, sardines and so on – will deteriorate quicker because the of high levels of unstable monounsaturated fats, so I would only store these fish for three months before consuming. That said, even if they are frozen, I prefer to eat fish as quickly as possible as the textures can soften and become unpleasantly spongy with time.

Squid, cuttlefish and octopus (the cephalopods) all freeze brilliantly and the freezing action serves to tenderize the meat, so it's a double win. I wouldn't freeze live shellfish – mussels, clams, and so on – but I would lightly steam to cook and open them, then pick the meat out and freeze it without the shells, freezing separately on a tray first, before scooping into a box or bag (so they don't clump together).

Crab, lobster, langoustine and prawns all freeze well, raw or cooked.

Frozen seafood should be thawed in the fridge and the thawing process is generally pretty speedy. You could, however, toss handfuls of cooked frozen mussels or clams into a pasta sauce or soup and they would defrost super-quick.

At the other end of the eating experience, should you find you have leftover cooked fish, that also freezes well. I often pick off bits and bobs from the frame (that's all the bones, head, tail fins – the whole structure of the fish), bag and freeze, and then, when I have accumulated enough, I use them to make Classic fishcakes (page 169), Celeriac and salt cod rosti (page 185) or Smoked fish and courgette pancakes (page 189). Little scraps of cured smoked fish also freeze well for another day and get used in the same way, or perhaps stirred into a simple pasta sauce.

BASIC FISH SKILLS

How much hands-on prep you want to do is your call, and a good fishmonger will do as much or as little as you like. They will, without a doubt, do it better than you or I can; they are the experts here and there is no shame in wanting to avoid the prep entirely, but I am quite a hands-on kind of cook so I do like buying my fish whole and getting stuck in.

Here are my thoughts and guidance on fish filleting. As with any of these nitty-gritty skills, it's often much easier to do than to explain to how to do. So a great place to start is just to practise, and as we all know, watching videos on YouTube is a marvellous thing for learning practical skills. Buy some inexpensive fish – mackerel in season perhaps – and just give it a go. The worst that can happen is your fillets are a little raggedy and you've not cleaned the flesh from the frame quite as much as you could have. It will still be entirely edible and delicious used in a recipe. And don't forget you can always scrape off the frame and freeze any little scraps for another day to use in recipes like the fishcakes on page 169.

For all shellfish, crustacean and cephalopod prep, head to the Suckers and Shells chapter (page 198).

How to scale a fish

Different fish have different-sized scales and unless they are big and obvious, I don't necessarily do anything to remove them, viewing them as another way of protecting the delicate skin from the fire. Once cooked, they add a little extra crispiness, too. Fish that have large or hard scales, like a bass, do benefit from having them removed. Your fishmonger may have done it for you, but if not, it's easy but a little messy.

I would first suss out my fish. If the scales look large – larger than, say, a big lentil – slide it into a plastic bag, then use the blunt back edge of a knife and scrape the skin from the tail end up towards the head end, flicking off the scales as you go. The scales are contained in the bag and you can remove and wipe the fish with paper towel and rest on a rack over a tray before carrying on with the drying stage in the fridge.

How to gut a fish

This may already have been done, as many fish, including pretty much all flatfish you can buy, will be gutted onboard the fishing boat. If it hasn't, this is what you do.

Make an incision into the anal vent – located about two-thirds of the way down the belly towards the tail end – with the tip of a very sharp knife. Cut upwards towards the head, stopping at the gills under the bottom jaw. You can snip through the jaw with scissors to fully open out the fish. Open up the cavity with your fingers and pull out the guts, which should come away in one piece. If they don't, grab a small knife or pair of scissors to help you. Wipe the empty cavity and skin really clean

with paper towel. I never wash fish or fillets in water, preferring to keep everything as dry as possible. This helps with the all-important sticking question and keeps the fish fresher for longer (page 16).

How to fillet a round fish

Pat the surface of the fish dry with paper towels to make it less slippery to hold. Lay the fish across a board with its back towards you and the head facing your dominant hand. Take the flat palm of your other hand to press and hold the fish down; creating a little pressure will firm up the flesh and make cutting easier and safer.

Make a cut round the back of the head down to the bone, curving the knife as close to the pectoral fin as possible, following the line of the gill flap. Angling the knife edge towards the tail, slice the flesh away as close to the bone as you can, opening it out a little. Then use a clean sweeping motion, rather than a sawing action, to slide the length of the knife all the way down the backbone towards the tail, keeping the blade as close to the bones as possible. Flip the fish over and repeat on the other side, beginning with the curved slice down round the pectoral fin. Keep applying pressure with the palm of your hand to hold the fish secure as you fillet.

Use fish tweezers to pinch out the pin bones that will be lurking along the centre line of each fillet, along with any rib bones that you missed as you cut the fillet off. Don't forget to save the frame and any trimmings for the stock pot, freezing them well wrapped in a bag if you don't have time immediately (page 16).

Skinning the fillets

Round fish are filleted before the skin is removed, and in many recipes here I wouldn't go on to remove the skin at all, preferring to use it to protect the delicate fillet and to get crispy and delicious to eat. If you were going on to wrap the fish in something – such as in Nori-wrapped cod (page 80) or Ling wrapped in fig leaves (page 104) – the skin would need to come off as it won't get a chance to go crispy, although in rare cases, it is too thin to remove.

Removing the skin is a pretty easy task, particularly on the thicker-skinned fish like haddock. Rest the fillet across a board with the tail end facing your less dominant hand and the thicker end facing your cutting hand. Add a good pinch of coarse salt to the tail end, then make a little nick down the flesh to the skin a few millimetres from the end. Using the gritty salt to help you grip, hold the tail tight with one hand and slide the knife between the skin and flesh towards the thick end of the fillet, with the blade of the knife angled down and almost parallel to the skin. It's a simultaneous tug with one hand and a sweeping motion with the knife in the other.

How to butterfly

Butterflying is simply opening the fish out flat by removing the backbone and ribs to give you a thin, even layer. It's a great technique to make cooking speedy and to give you an all-important large surface area to contact with the hot grill for maximum crispy skin.

To butterfly, you need a fish with the guts intact. If the fish is already gutted, try the reverse butterfly overleaf.

Pat the fish dry with paper towel so it's more grippy. If you are right-handed, start with the fish on a board with its head towards your left hand and its belly facing your own body. (If you are left-handed, reverse the direction of flow.) Hold the fish firmly with the flat palm of your left hand. Use a knife in your right hand to cut around the fish's head down to the bone, curving all the way round the pectoral fin. Flip the fish over and repeat the cut, then make a snip with scissors to break the head off the backbone. You should now be able to pick the fish up and, holding the body in one hand and the head in the other, twist off the head and pull out the guts in one move.

Then lay the fish with its tail towards you, backbone to the right, and draw the knife down the backbone from the head end down to the tail. Deepen the cut, slicing down across the ribs towards the belly but taking care not to pierce the belly. Open up the fillet, then flip the fish over so it is frame-side down, tail away from you and repeat along the other side of the backbone.

Use scissors to snip away the frame, leaving you with a kite-shaped fillet with the tail on. Use tweezers to remove pin bones and rib bones. As above, save the frame and trimmings for the stock pot.

How to reverse butterfly
Reverse butterflying is just the opposite way round, so you remove the backbone via the belly cavity rather than by slicing along the spine. The head gets left on and is opened out flat – I guess a little like spatchcocking a chicken.

Start with a conventionally gutted fish, patting it dry to make the skin easier to grip. Rest the fish on a board, spine down, with the head facing towards you and the tail furthest from you. Take a sharp pair of scissors, insert through the gut cavity and snip down one side of the spine, inserting the tip of the scissor blades between the backbone and ribs. Snip down the other side, then use the scissors to cut through the spine at the tail and head end. Cut through the jaw so you can flatten the head, then gently remove the spine, pulling carefully with your fingers so you don't tear the skin. Finally, use fish tweezers to pull out the rib and pin bones.

How to 'canoe' or pocket bone
Canoe or pocket boning is similar to butterflying in that you remove the backbone from the back rather than reverse butterflying (where the backbone is removed via the belly). However, you are not cutting off the head or tail and not flattening it out, so you are left with a whole, boneless fish that has a canoe-shaped pocket that you can stuff with tasty things before roasting.

You need a whole, intact, ungutted fish. Pat the fish dry with paper towels and rest it belly-side down on a board with the tail facing you and the head furthest away from you. Use a sharp knife to slice down one side of the backbone from a centimetre further down than the back of the head to about a centimetre before the tail. Only slice down a little lower than the spine – about 5mm or so, so you don't pierce into the belly. Repeat on the other side of the backbone, then take scissors and snip through the backbone at the head and tail ends. Gently pull the backbone out and using fingers to work the flesh off the rib bones. Gently pull away the guts, taking care not to pierce the belly skin. Wipe the cavity well with paper towels, then stuff as desired, such as the Mackerel 'canoe' stuffed with spiced currant rice (page 72).

ESSENTIAL KIT FOR FISH PREPARATION

To deal with a whole fish effectively you need a few bits of kit.

A filleting knife

This is a sharp knife with a thin, slightly flexible, curved blade that you can angle close to the bone and follow the line of the fish's frame. No one ever filleted a fish well with a blunt knife so you will also need something to keep it sharp, and sharpen it often.

Scissors

Just standard kitchen scissors are super helpful for trimming off fins and snipping through ribs and backbones.

Fish tweezers

These have a broad, flat end you can use to grasp pin bones effectively. Your eyebrow tweezers probably won't cut it – I know because I've tried! – as they generally have too fine an end to grip a slippery bone.

To use fish tweezers, rest the fish fillet with the tail end pointing towards your non-dominant hand, and run that hand lightly across the fillet from the head end to the tail end, feeling for bones, working against the direction they are lying. Then use the tweezers in your dominant hand to firmly pull out the bones, working with the flow of the bone, so pulling towards the head end. It's a fiddly, time-consuming job but quite mindful in its own way if you accept the vibe of it.

Your fingers

Actually I find these are some of the best tools for home filleting. You can often use your fingers to ease flesh away from bones in a more delicate, gentle way than with a knife so I often put my knife down and use my hands during the process. I once watched bush craft legend Ray Mears fillet a whole large salmon using nothing more than his bare hands. Mesmerizing, to say the least.

BARBECUE HARDWARE

What you choose to cook on, or your 'hardware', can be a very simple choice for seafood because it cooks quickly and doesn't generally (unless it's a large, whole fish) benefit from having a lid to trap in convection heat. Therefore a fairly basic set-up – even a metal bucket with an old grill rack – will often do the job just fine. You certainly don't need very expensive Kamado-style ovens or offset smokers for fish cooking, although you can cook and smoke fish in these very well if you happen to have them.

All the recipes in this book were cooked either on my beloved Weber kettle, or on an open fire table, and you'll see pictures of both scattered throughout the pages. My fire table was made by Netherton Foundry and it is sturdy and brilliant to cook on.

A barbecue oven

If you want to turn your barbecue into an oven – for example, if you want to bake the Smoked fish pie (page 166) or the Fishage rolls (page 195) – you need to create an environment where convection heat rules and you knock out all infra-red heat and most conduction heat (we'll go into these three types of heat when we start the fire – read on!). The easiest way to do this is to light two small fires on either side of the barbecue and place the food in between them. Of course, to create an oven you need a lid to trap the hot air in; after all, you wouldn't try to bake a cake in the oven and leave the door open.

Temperature probe

Fish is cooked within a very narrow temperature range of only around 5°C (9°F), so it is easy to undercook, or much more commonly, overcook. It's easier to visually tell when fillets of fish are cooked as you can clearly see the flakes, but the situation is harder when the fish is whole and the skin hides the flesh, or when the fish is wrapped in something, such as Leek-wrapped cod (page 109). So, just as with meat cooking, I would consider my temperature probe to be an essential bit of kit. It just takes any guesswork away and gives you, the cook, confidence in the doneness. As a reminder, fish is cooked when the internal temperature reaches 60°C (140°F). Providing you are not vulnerable or immunocompromised, it is safe to eat fish less well cooked, just as you might eat a beef steak rare. Tuna is a good example of when you might actively choose to cook to a lower internal temperature (page 76).

Trays and racks for drying

Throughout these recipes you will see me refer to resting the fish over a rack on a tray. It's a technique I deploy time and again because the principal enemy of fish cooking – sticking – is exacerbated by a wet surface. I have some sturdy stainless steel racks I found online at the retailing behemoth we all love to hate. Try Googling 'baking trays with racks'; they are very handy for all sorts of fish and meat cooking.

Grill trays and fish cages

Perforated grill trays, as seen on page 89, are one of the most useful bits of kit in my arsenal, letting in the smoky goodness of the fire but giving you, the cook, more control. Fish is a delicate protein and it's very useful to be able to remove it from the barbecue completely to turn, rotate or unstick it during cooking. It can be a bit fiddly so the last thing you want to do is do it over the heat – letting out the hot air while fuelling the fire with more oxygen is just going to speed up the rate that the fuel gets burnt.

A fish cage is a double-sided rack that you then insert the fish in between, first getting it super-hot to help prevent sticking. I find them frustrating, often being the wrong shape for the fish in question, or the wrong shape for my barbecue or just not of a great design. I have one with a surface coiled like mattress springs and it is appalling for sticking; needless to say I only used it once. They often have long handles that get in the way, too, meaning that you can't rest them fully onto the grill bars. Something with simple straight lines and no handle is much better, and you just use tongs to turn it. I still haven't found the 'perfect' fish cage and one day I will try to design my own.

With fillets, or smaller whole fish, I would reach for a grill tray first, and if I were cooking a whole larger fish that would be tricky to turn with a fish slice – like a turbot – then I would use a fish cage.

Pots, pans, trays

In many recipes you will see me say to take a flameproof pan or pot to the fire. All I mean by that is no plastic or wooden handles, and not non-stick. Apart from that, pretty much anything goes. I take all my inside kitchen kit outside to my fire. That said, things will develop a certain 'patina' from fire cooking, so the outside may discolour a little from the high heat and smoke. I like it! It's like a badge of honour, but if you have anything particularly precious, just choose something else. I am particularly keen on those enamel tins – the white and blues ones – they are lightweight, cheap and cheerful.

Fish weights

I've written more on these on page 75 as these are more relevant to the Bits of Fish chapter. In essence, these are heavy things to stop fillets curling up as you cook them.

Odds and ends

Plus, you'll need the usual fire-cooking suspects for all outside cooking, not just fish.

Thick gloves: These will protect your hands and forearms from the heat. (Just as with fish cages, I have never found the perfect pair. One day I will design my own.)

Long-handled tongs: Tongs should have just the right amount of tension you feel comfortable with. I like my tongs fairly loose so I can use them without too much grip. Some tongs are really hard to squeeze, which reduces my efficiency in turning and creates extra unnecessary effort.

One fish slice, two fish slices: Invaluable for turning, and sometimes two are better than one.

A chimney starter: The best way to get charcoal lit quickly and efficiently. See page 31 for lighting fires.

Natural firelighters: I only ever use wood-twists dipped in wax to start my fires, and with a well-laid wood fire or a chimney starter, you will only need one per fire.

If you are going to try smoking some fish, you'll need a couple of extra items (head to Chapter 4).

How to clean your barbecue

I use nothing but heat and a stiff wire brush to clean the inside of my barbecue. By the time you have lit charcoal, burning as it does at around 500°C (932°F), heat is by far the best form of sterilization and way better than any kind of detergent. Make sure you check your wire brush regularly and replace with a new one should any wires start shedding.

HOW TO COOK FISH

Understanding why a food reacts in relation to heat will help you get the best results. The first, almost the only, question I am ever asked about cooking fish is, 'but how do I stop it from sticking?!' It's the perennial question, and one I can definitely help a little with, but before that it's super-helpful to explore how fish differs from meat.

Differences between land and sea

Fish proteins are arranged differently than land animal proteins so they behave differently on cooking. They are shorter and arranged in 'blocks' stacked alongside each other in distinct layers, a bit like rows of bricks with thin sheets of connective tissue in between, which we can clearly witness as delicate 'flakes' of cooked fish. This allows the fish to move, wave-like, as it swims. By contrast, meat protein fibres are much longer and arranged in bundles, which we see as more strand-like when cooked, for example as in the texture of pulled pork.

The connective tissues and fats that flow between the protein blocks are chemically different too. Fish need to function at way lower temperatures than land animals so their fat is fluid and, just like olive oil, it is unsaturated, so that they can swim in cold water. If their bodies were loaded with solid saturated fat, like beef, for example, they wouldn't be able to move in the water; they would be rigid.

These differences, without going into too much geeky detail, mean that fish flesh breaks down and is cooked at lower internal temperatures than meat. It also means the temperature range between 'raw' and 'done' is very narrow, just 5°C (9°F) or so. Which all goes to explain why it is prone to falling apart and easy to overcook. Fish is cooked at 60°C (140°F), a few degrees either side is raw or overdone. With meat, you get a bigger margin to play with, from about 50°C (122°F) in a rather rare steak, to often over 100°C (212°F) in a smoked brisket.

All about sticking

The nature of fish protein – it's a delicate protein that cooks fast – also means that it tends to be sticky and prone to falling apart. We can do a lot to minimize the impact of this and there are several key elements at play.

Dryness of the fish surface: You need to minimize as much of the water on the fish's surface as possible, which is why the majority of the recipes here will begin by asking you to rest your fish on a wire rack hung over a tray for a few hours before you cook it. It really, really helps so do try to plan a few hours ahead of cooking.

The cleanliness of the cooking surface: You need to make sure the grill bars, the fish cage or the grill tray are squeaky clean, so trays and cages should be washed as you would wash any roasting pan, for example, and grill bars should be burned hot with the fire and scrubbed well with a wire brush before you cook.

A HOT cooking surface: This needs to be really very hot. If you put a cold fish in a cold fish cage and set it on a hot fire, it will stick. Put a cold fish in a hot cage – it should literally sizzle as you rest it in – it will stick a lot less. It's that simple.

A properly, fully hot fire to cook over: Head to page 28 for more on the fire, but briefly I have found that a fire to cook fish well needs to have burnt hot and fully to embers, and then you cook on those embers as they burn down from their peak heat.

Timing the turn: Don't try to turn the fish too soon or the skin will tear. You want to develop a good crispy skin before you move it. Tease a corner with a fish slice and, if it feels stuck, cook for another 30 seconds or so before trying again.

Sea salt: Sprinkling the skin generously with flaked sea salt before cooking also helps to reduce sticking as you create a lovely crunchy little barrier between skin and grill bars.

Lastly, I think perhaps we will need to relax and roll with it a little. This is home cooking rather than Michelin fine dining. So what if we end up with a little tear in the skin here or there, or that we may need to shove and push (a move known as the 'gronch' in our house!) the fish slice to release the fillet free with a little more vigour than is 'perfect'? Will it still taste great? Of that I have no doubt.

General cooking notes

- **Toasting spices**: In all the recipes in this book that use spices, I suggest you buy them whole and toast them briefly before using in the recipes. This may seem like a small, skippable step but I urge you to do it. A little gentle heat will 'wake up' the aromatic flavour compounds in the spices and just make them taste more spicy. It's an invaluable flavour-boosting trick that takes less than a minute.

- **Salt**: I always use Maldon flaked sea salt for general seasoning.

- **Olive oil**: I favour using a pretty standard extra virgin olive oil for practically everything I cook, unless it's an Asian dish where I substitute rapeseed or sesame. Good olive oil is one of life's great pleasures so I save a more special extra virgin oil for dressings and post-cooking drizzles. If I will willingly sip it off a spoon, I will drizzle it with abandon. Think of all those good polyphenols flowing into your body.

FIRE BASICS

A lot of recipes here are not instantly what you might think of as 'barbecue' recipes. I very much see my barbecue, and the heat generated by the lit charcoal or wood, as just another cooking source. With a little knowledge of fire and the physics of heat, it is quite easy to turn your barbecue from grill to hob to oven. Often the act of cooking outside is reason enough for me to light my fire, it doesn't matter if I'm traditionally 'barbecuing' or not.

Of course, on the flip side of this is the rather useful fact that you can easily take almost everything in this book, with the exception of the smoked things, and cook it inside your kitchen should the weather, or the energy levels, dictate a vibe of 'can I really be bothered?'. Trust me, I cook with fire practically every day, but occasionally I just can't be arsed either. Cooking something good to eat shouldn't be a chore.

What is fire?

A basic physics lesson is useful here, so even if you think you hate physics, a quick read may help make fire cooking magically fall into place.

Fire is just the heat source. Combustion, the chemical reaction we know as fire, needs three things to make it happen: **fuel, a spark** and **oxygen**. For fuel we are using charcoal and/or wood, the spark is a match, and the oxygen comes by way of air.

The impact of oxygen

I always think oxygen is the one we play with to impact how the heat of our fire works. With more oxygen, you get a quicker, hotter fire and with less oxygen you get a cooler, more gentle fire. So by using the air vents to control the oxygen flow on a lidded barbecue we can control the temperature. If you are feeling curious you can do a home experiment to witness the power of the oxygen. Light a fire in your barbecue, shut the lid and moderate the vents down to give you a nice gentle heat. Let it stabilize for a while, then raise the lid and stand there watching the charcoal. It will pretty quickly be glowing hot and red, burning quicker, hotter and more efficiently.

The impact of fuel

The amount of fuel we start with also has an impact, so if you want a more gentle heat, starting with less fuel is a good beginning. Two handfuls of charcoal could give us twice the heat energy potential as one handful. Get used to the fuel you use and learn how much of it you need to cook a meal with. Very often people use far too much fuel and then are left with a fire the burns on for way longer than it takes to cook your food, wasting energy (and money).

Fire creates three kinds of heat.

Infra-red heat: This is radiation, the 'mother heat', the actual heat generated from the burning fuel. If we are cooking directly, we cook over the fire and use this heat. With fully combusting charcoal you can expect to have a heat of over 500°C (932°F) coming off it, so really very hot. Fish doesn't necessarily need this amount of fierce heat, so head to page 31 for a description of what I'd call a good 'fish fire'.

Conduction heat: Infra-red heat quickly transfers into anything conductible, so generally anything metal in a standard barbecue: the grill bars, the lid, any grill cages or fish trays you might put in. They get hot, then you put cold food onto the hot surface and the heat energy transfers into the food, and the food cooks. With time, the grill bars directly over the fire will equalize in temperature to the lit charcoal, so you could get a heat of 500°C (932°F) on them, whereas the grill bars off to the side of the fire will get incrementally cooler the further you travel from the source heat. With this concept in mind, we can create different 'heat zones', which are extremely useful for giving us temperature control.

Convection heat: The last heat is hot air, remarkably efficient at cooking – and how your fan oven works in the kitchen – as long as you can shut the lid to trap it in. Convection heat is much less important with seafood because as it cooks so quickly, you rarely need to create that oven-like heat; a one-directional heat from underneath is all you need. Where convection becomes important is hot smoking, and in that chapter – or anywhere else you need convection heat, baking the fish pie on page 166, for example – you will see me refer to shutting the lid to trap the heat and the smoke in.

What temperature should my barbecue be?

This is a very common question and I do think people can get a little hung up on it. It just doesn't give you the whole 'thermal picture', only telling you a third of the story. The lid temperature gauge is only measuring one thing: the convection heat, the hot air. It gives you no idea about the infra-red or conduction heat.

So the lid temperature is only relevant if you are cooking with the lid down, and even then only partly relevant because it's as much to do with where the food is in relation to the infra-red radiation – or the 'mother heat' – as to what temperature the lid says.

Charcoal or wood, what is best?

Charcoal burns hotter than wood, two to three times hotter, and it's a more even, consistent product because it is essentially pure carbon. Wood burns less hot and creates smoke, each log burns slightly differently, as does each species of tree. So wood is more variable to cook on.

Because seafood cooks quickly cooking on an open fire, with no lid, using either charcoal or wood is just as effective a heat source. Wood will naturally give you a little more 'character' and flavour to your food because of the smoke it generates.

How to light a charcoal fire

A chimney starter is the quickest way to light
a charcoal fire. With good charcoal (please buy
it, page 12) and a chimney, the coals can be ready
to cook on in less than 10 minutes. Simply fill
the chimney with charcoal with a single natural
firelighter (page 24) underneath. The firelighter
generates a little heat, which pulls in the air around.
That air and the flame whoosh up through the
charcoal and in no time it will be lit and ready
to tip into your barbecue and get cooking.

How to light a wood fire

With wood, I always light a top-down fire. It's such
an effective way to light a fire I am almost evangelical
about it. You build a neat, structurally stable 'Jenga'
stack of logs, place a little kindling on top and set a
natural firelighter on top of that. Light the firelighter
and the flame will quickly catch the kindling alight.
The hot embers from the kindling will fall down and
light the next layer in the stack, which in turn lights
the layer below. I find this the absolute best way to
light a fire even if it feels a little counterintuitive at
first. The combustion process, involving the fuel,
spark and oxygen, is at its most efficient, meaning
less smoke (and therefore pollution) as the fire
gets going.

What sort of fire for cooking seafood?

When you light a fire, it goes through different
stages of combustion; fire has a clear life cycle.
In the beginning, the heat is rising as the fire takes
hold. Flame itself is not great for cooking on, it's
a sooty and not particularly hot heat, so the only
time I would consider cooking over live flame is
if I had food protected in a pan – starting off a sauce,
for example. Once the fuel has all burned with flames,
you are left with intensely hot embers, which is when
the fire is at its hottest. The embers then reduce
gently in temperature as the fuel burns away.

You can do a lot of cooking on the rising heat of
burning embers as they come up to their maximum
heat energy, but I have learnt that the best fire
for cooking seafood is a fire that is just beginning

to drop off the maximum and is starting the
downward trajectory from its peak. Throughout this
book you will see me refer to cooking fish over fully
burned embers. The rising heat is where you start
cooking sauces, vegetable accompaniments and
so on, then once the embers have reached maximum
heat and are just starting to drop off, that is when
you cook the fish.

It is also worth noting here that the amount of fuel
you need to use may not be as much as you think.
The nature of fish protein means it cooks very quickly
(head back to page 26 for a refresh), so you don't need
a lot of fuel to get your dinner to the table. However,
what you do need is a thin even bed of embers that
pretty much matches exactly the area of the fish you
are cooking. This way the whole fish, or whole fillet,
cooks at the same time thus avoiding over-done and
under-done parts. So even if the recipe calls for other
elements to be cooked as the fire heats up – a sauce
in a pan for example – make sure that when you are
ready to get the fish on you have spread your embers
out to an appropriate size.

Fire set-ups

Regardless of what you cook on, knowing the
difference between **direct** and **indirect** cooking
is a critical skill. Quite simply, with direct cooking,
the food is above the fire, and with indirect
cooking, the food is off the side of the fire. With
all fire cooking, you always want to have heat in
one part of your barbecue and no heat in the other,
so even if a recipe calls for hot direct cooking, you
have a cooler zone to move things to if the food
looks like it is burning. This gives us, the cooks,
heat control and is pretty much the founding
principle of better grilling.

So, when you are starting to cook and lighting your
fire, think about the area the fish is going to take up
on the grill. You will need an area of about the same
size to grill your fish over, but wherever possible leave
a space to one side of that so you can move the fish
over there should things look like they are getting
too hot.

FISH STOCKS

I'm always pretty tight when it comes to cooking seafood. It's not only expensive to buy, but also a precious natural resource not to be squandered. So in plenty of places you will see me mention making stock from bones, or freezing trimmings from filleting or slicing cured fish, squirrelling away bits of this and that to use in recipes another day. You can find some ideas for using up little bits of fish in Mackerel, leek and horseradish fishage rolls (page 195), Smoked fish and courgette pancakes (page 189) or Classic fishcakes (page 169).

I also often make stock from bits and pieces and here are three variations plus a crab shell bisque that tastes anything but frugal. If you have asked the fishmonger to do the filleting job for you, don't forget to ask for the frames, skin, heads and tails in a bag. After all, you've paid for them and you can always bung them into your freezer when you get home to make stock another day.

Light fish stock

This is a classic, infinitely adaptable, fish stock recipe. Here I have stuck to the trinity of carrots, celery and onion, but you could easily add other bits and bobs you might have lurking around – leek trimmings, fennel or mushroom stalks would all be good. Try different herbs, too – maybe oregano, dill or tarragon.

As for the fish? Well, you can pretty much use any white fish bones you have, aiming for around 750g (1lb 10oz) in weight, although even this isn't critical. The more bones (or 'frames' as they are known), the stronger the stock will be. Heads, tails and trimmings are all good, too, although I would always remove and discard the gills (the dark red frilly bits under the gill flaps) as they are bitter. If I don't have enough bones, or am not in a stock-making mood, I just freeze them ready for when stock-making is on my agenda. Also, it's worth adding that I make stock either from raw bones post filleting, or I make stock from cooked bones, just scooping them up once we've eaten the fish. If you are worried about the hygiene of making stock from bones that may have been on various people's plates, remember that they get boiled up for 30 minutes so there are really no worries on this front.

Put the butter in a large stock pot and set over a medium–low heat on the hob to melt. Tip in the carrots, celery and onion and add the bay leaves, thyme, parsley, salt and peppercorns. Sweat the vegetables for a generous 20–30 minutes, stirring occasionally. You are not looking to colour them but soften and intensify their flavours.

Once soft, add the fish frames, then turn up the heat and pour in enough cold water to cover completely by about 1cm (½in) and bring up to the boil. Add the wine, if using, and reduce the heat to a steady simmer and cook for 30 minutes.

Hang a sieve over a large bowl and strain the stock through it. Discard the solids.

At this point you can cool, chill and store in the fridge. It will stay fresh for 3–5 days. Or you can bag and freeze. If you are short on freezer space, another option is to put the strained stock back into a clean pan and reduce it right down, then freeze as a concentrated liquid. Whether you freeze at full volume or a reduced concentrated version, the stock will keep for 3 months.

Makes about 1 litre (34fl oz/4 cups)

75g (2½oz) butter
2 carrots, finely chopped
2 celery stalks, finely chopped
1 onion or leek, finely chopped
2 bay leaves
a few sprigs of thyme
a few stems of parsley
1 tsp flaked sea salt
1 tbsp black peppercorns
about 750g (1lb 10oz) white
    fish frames and trimmings,
    chopped into 6–10cm
    (2½–4in) pieces
a generous splash of white wine,
    about 3–5 tbsp (optional)

Rich fish stock

There is an oft-quoted 'rule' that you can't make a fish stock from oily fish like salmon, mackerel or sardines. I'm here to tell you that you can. What you get is a much richer, I guess oilier, end product, deeply flavoursome and intense and not bad in any way, just different, and really great to use as a base for richer fish dishes, such as the Black rice with grilled cuttlefish and aioli (page 250) or Monkfish and chard paella (page 248) for example. If the extra oil is bothersome, you could chill it down then skim it off in the same way you might with a beef stock, although I think it's way better to view it as an excellent nutritional addition for your health.

The basic method here is very similar to the Light fish stock (page 33) except in this one I get the frames, heads and trimmings in the stock pot first and try to get a little colour into them, at the same time rendering out some of their oils that will add depth of flavour and also help soften the veg.

Due to the high oil content, this stock doesn't store as well as a white fish stock. If you are freezing it, I suggest you use it within a month.

Put the fish frames into a large stock pot and set over a high heat on the hob. Fry, stirring every now and then, until they release some of their oils and take on a little colour. Then add the celery, carrots, onion and herbs, along with the salt and peppercorns. Turn down the heat and allow the veg to soften in the fish oils for around 15 minutes, stirring occasionally.

Turn up the heat and pour in enough cold water to cover everything by a good 1cm (½in). Bring up to the boil, add the sherry, if using, then reduce the heat to a steady simmer and cook for 30 minutes.

Hang a sieve over a large bowl and strain the stock through it, discarding the solids. Allow to cool, then store in the fridge and use within 3–5 days or freeze for up to a month.

Makes about 1 litre (34fl oz/4 cups)

about 750g (1lb 10oz) fish frames and trimmings from trout, salmon or mackerel, chopped into 6–10cm (2½–4in) pieces
3 celery stalks, finely chopped
2 large carrots, finely chopped
1 onion, finely chopped
4 bay leaves
a handful of thyme, marjoram or oregano
a few sprigs of parsley
1 tsp flaked sea salt
1 tbsp black peppercorns
a generous splash of dry sherry, about 3–5 tbsp (optional)

Shellfish stock

Another example of an intense stock best used for dishes that fall into the more full-on end of the fishy spectrum; try it in the Cambodian-style fish curry (page 259), the Monkfish and chard paella (page 248) or the Crab and tarragon bisque (page 37).

I use a couple of brown crab shells and legs in this recipe, but you could use the shells and leftover trimmings from spider crab, lobster, langoustine or prawns. Just don't add any gills as they can add a bitter note. Quantities or weights of shells isn't specific. If you have more, the stock will be stronger and less will be more subtle.

Wrap the shells loosely in a clean dish towel and bash with a rolling pin to break up into pieces – you don't need to go wild, 2cm (¾in) pieces are fine. Take a large stockpot and add the shell fragments, along with the onion, garlic, tomato purée and peppercorns. Add the cold water and set over a medium heat on the hob. Bring to the boil, cover with a lid and reduce the heat to a simmer. Cook for 1 hour, then strain the stock through a fine sieve into a bowl. Chill for 3 days or freeze for up to 3 months until required.

Makes about 1 litre (34fl oz/4 cups)

2 brown crab shells and legs, and all the bits apart from the gills and guts
1 onion, chopped
2 garlic cloves, bruised
1 tbsp tomato purée (paste)
1 tsp black peppercorns
1 litre (34fl oz/4 cups) water

Crab and tarragon bisque

Here is something delicious and easy to do with your shellfish stock. I made this using a crab-shell base in the Shellfish stock (page 35) but it would work equally well with a prawn, lobster, crayfish or langoustine stock. If you are using a different shell base, you may not have handy access to the crab meat element, although I urge you to try the Grilled spider or brown crab legs (page 241) and save a little meat for this. You could sub in a little lobster, crayfish or prawn flesh or, for that taste that only brown crab meat gives you, grab a little ready-picked crab from the fishmonger or supermarket.

Set a generous heavy-based pan onto the hob over a low heat and melt the butter. Add the celeriac, onion, carrot, tarragon and chilli, if using. Season generously with salt and pepper and cook really gently for a generous 20–30 minutes until the vegetables are really soft but not coloured. Pour in the whisky or brandy and raise the heat a little to allow it to bubble off, then pour in the stock. Bring to the boil and simmer steadily for another 20 minutes or so.

Remove from the heat and stir through most of the crab meat and the double cream and sprinkle over the cornflour. Use a stick blender in the pan to purée until completely smooth, then set back over a low heat to thicken for 5 minutes or so, stirring occasionally.

Pour into warmed soup bowls and sprinkle over a little reserved tarragon and the remaining crab meat just before serving. If you were feeling fancy, you could top with an extra swirl of double cream.

Serves 4–6

50g (2oz) butter
250g (9oz) celeriac, chopped into 1–2cm (½–¾in) chunks
1 large red onion, finely chopped
1 carrot, chopped
a handful of tarragon, leaves picked and roughly chopped (reserve a little to garnish)
a pinch of chilli (hot pepper) flakes (optional)
2 tbsp whisky or brandy
1 quantity of Shellfish stock (page 35), about 800ml (28fl oz/3½ cups)
100g (3½oz) crab meat, a mix of white and brown
150ml (5fl oz/scant ⅔ cup) double (heavy) cream (perhaps add 100ml (3½fl oz/ scant ½ cup), then garnish with the reminder if you wish)
1 heaped tbsp cornflour (cornstarch)
flaked sea salt and freshly ground black pepper

Chapter 1:
The Whole Fish

A whole fish, grilled simply and eaten under warm sunny skies – I'm really not sure if barbecue gets any better and it was this vision, this memory of summer-holiday fish, that kick-started this whole book.

Over and above the obvious eating joys, cooking a whole fish has other benefits. Most of the fat lies in and under the fish's skin, which is where it is at its most succulent and nutritious. That is going to protect the more delicate flesh while it is cooking, help prevent it sticking and prevent the muscle drying out. With a careful read of the recipes you'll note that I never ask you to cut slashes through the skin into the flesh. This was something I always used to do but have learnt on this journey that intact whole skin is simply better. If you cut the skin, you introduce a weakness, an area more prone to sticking and tearing, whereas if the skin is whole you stand a better chance of achieving the end goal, which is skin so crisp you can't help but eat it. No one likes the texture of floppy fish skin, but cooked properly, it is surely where the goodness lies.

The principles of all good fish cooking – that is dry skin and a hot, steady bed of embers – stands firm for all the recipes in this chapter, so do head back for a refresh on the basics. Try your best not to skip the drying step – it's genuinely important, so give yourself enough time to do it properly. With a whole fish you can dry for longer than a small fillet as the flesh is protected by the skin, so think 12–24 hours ahead if you can.

How to serve a whole fish

A whole fish is something I would cook for my nearest and dearest, preferring to slide it onto a dish and into the centre of the table so that each guest can just grab little portions for their own plates, heading back in for seconds as often as they want. I enjoy informal eating, which is probably why barbecue floats my boat so much. No one ever feels the need to stand on ceremony when you are cooking (and hopefully eating, weather permitting) outside.

However, if you want to 'carve' whole fish at the table in a more formal way – and my kids certainly prefer to eat fish like this – then you need nothing more than a table knife and fork, as cooked fish is super-delicate so no sharp knives are needed.

Start with the fish resting on a plate and use the cutlery to pull away the fin bones on the dorsal (top) and ventral (bottom) sides.

Then cut around the fillet where it meets the head, curving the cut around the gill flap so you don't miss the chunky nugget of flesh near the top of the head. Cut through the tail end down to the bone, then draw the knife along the centre of the fillet, following the mid line where the spine is all the way up to the head. Run the table knife under the flesh from the centre out to the back as close to the bones as possible to release the top, dorsal, half of the fillet. Run the knife in the other direction to release the bottom, ventral, half of the fillet. Now you should be able to pull away the frame, head and tail included, to leave the underside fillet intact. You may need to give it a scrape to remove any bits of membrane or bones that have stuck.

1. **Head**
2. **Gill Flap**
3. **Dorsal Fillet**
4. **Dorsal Fin**
5. **Mid Line**
6. **Ventral Fillet**
7. **Ventral Fin**
8. **Tail**

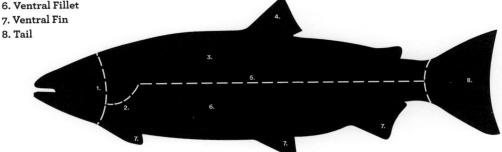

Flatfish

'Flatties' are brilliant fish for the barbecue and always best, I think, cooked whole. By their very nature, the fillets are thin (and pretty flat, of course) so prone to both falling apart and overcooking. Flatfish are always gutted on board the fishing boat so this is a job you would never have to undertake unless, of course, you have caught your own.

I give you four flatfish recipes here, two using plaice and megrim (or Cornish) sole that are pretty economical, and a couple of the big hitters – turbot and brill – that will involve you digging deep into your pockets for a special treat. All four recipes are somewhat interchangeable, so if you are feeling strapped but fancy the anchovy butter, just make it for dousing a grilled megrim or plaice. Or if payday has hit (hurrah!) but you don't like anchovies, try the green butter instead. It all works.

There are other varieties of sole to look out for, too – lemon, Dover, dab – all worth checking out. The biology of flatfish is really fascinating but probably best saved for your own research otherwise I'll run out of room for recipes, but suffice to say, their bottom-dwelling habits make them vulnerable to rather more destructive trawling methods. So try to seek out mature-sized fish that will have had a chance to complete a breeding season and ask your fishmonger about fishing methods that avoid an undersized catch (page 8). Halibut, another of the big, expensive flatfish, is not included in this book as they are highly unsustainable as a wild-caught species and there no longer exists any farmed options in the UK.

Fish cages, a love/hate relationship

As I explained earlier (page 24), I have yet to find the perfect fish cage to use on my barbecue, but for flatfish they really are the best thing to use; the fish's large surface area makes it pretty tricky to use a fish slice, or even two fish slices, to turn mid-cook. When you use a fish cage, it is vital to get it very hot before you put the fish anywhere near it. Don't attempt to cook a cold fish in a cold fish cage; it will stick for sure. Again, there's more detail aplenty in the introduction (page 26). Due to differences in the thicknesses of top and bottom fillets, if you are cooking two or more smaller flatfish, make sure you cook them all the same side up so they grill evenly.

Don't forget the stock!

Flatfish bones, along with the head and thick collagen-dense skin, make rather exceptional fish stock, so make sure you save them and freeze them once you have prepared the fish. Keep them well wrapped and add to them until you have enough to make a stock; they will keep happily for up to six months. Head back to the introduction (page 32) for detail on making stock, remembering that a good fish stock needs something like equal weights of fish to water for the best flavour.

Whole grilled plaice with green butter

This dish is utter fish simplicity: just fish, butter, herbs and some smoky goodness. Plaice is one of my favourite fish, not only for its delicate flavour but also as a great choice for both economy and sustainability.

The butter is great on pretty much any fish you fancy grilling. It freezes like a dream, so make plenty and freeze what you don't use – well wrapped it will keep for 3 months or so. Don't be constrained by your choice of herbs either. Basil, parsley, chives, tarragon, coriander (cilantro), a single herb or a blend – go for whatever you fancy or have to hand. Remember to save or freeze the fish frames ready for making stock.

Rest the plaice on a rack over a tray and slide into the fridge to air dry for a few hours, up to 12 or so will be fine (page 23).

Take a small bowl and mash up the butter with the herbs, garlic and salt and pepper. Scoop onto a piece of greaseproof (waxed) paper and roll up onto a log of about 3cm (1¼in) in diameter. Chill until needed.

When you are ready to cook, light the barbecue ready for hot direct grilling (page 31). Rest a fish cage over the fire to heat up and let the coals fully ignite and burn to embers. Make sure the embers take up the same amount of space as the fish will, so it cooks evenly; spread them out if necessary.

Remove the fish from the fridge and drizzle lightly all over with the olive oil. Sprinkle the fish generously with the salt on both sides and take to the barbecue.

Carefully lift the hot fish cage off the grill bars and add the fish, keeping them both the same way up. Rest the cage on the grill bars over the fire and cook for a few minutes on each side until the skin is lightly blistered and, using a temperature probe, the internal temperature in the deepest part of the fish is 55°C (131°F). Remove the cage and use a fish slice to release the fish from the cage, sliding it dark-side up onto a warmed platter.

Cut the butter into slices and dot over the fish, then loosely cover with foil. Take to a warm place – so into the kitchen rather than outside – and leave to rest for about 10 minutes or so until the temperature of the fish has increased to 60°C (140°F) before serving.

Serves 2

2 whole plaice, about 300g (10½oz) each
olive oil, to drizzle
1 tbsp flaked sea salt

For the green butter

100g (3½oz) butter, slightly softened
a good handful of soft green herbs, about 25g (¾oz), chopped
1 garlic clove, crushed to a paste
flaked sea salt and freshly ground black pepper

Cornish sole with browned shrimp butter

I love Cornish sole, or megrim as they are also known. They have rough, thick skin that can feel a little chewy to eat but the good news is it makes them less prone to sticking than many other fish, and underneath the skin the flesh is sweet and tasty. The butter here feels a little 'fancy' in a proper old-school restaurant kind of way, but it is supremely tasty and very easy to make. You can find cooked brown shrimps at your fishmongers or in bigger supermarkets.

Rest the fish on a rack over a tray and slide into the fridge to air dry for a few hours (page 23).

When you are ready to cook, light the barbecue with the coals piled to one side of the grill. Set a fish cage over the fire to heat up. Allow the charcoal to burn fully (page 31) before you start cooking, spreading the embers out to a size equal to the fish.

Take a small flameproof pan and set it directly over the fire. Drop in the butter and add the bay leaves, mace and a good grind of salt and pepper. Swirl the pan around a little as the butter melts and allow it to caramelize and brown, it should smell nutty and awesome. Drop in the shrimps and stir briefly before sliding the pan off the heat to keep warm.

Remove the fish from the fridge and drizzle lightly with olive oil, brushing it all over, then sprinkle with the salt over both sides.

Carefully lift the hot fish cage off the grill and add the fish, making sure both fish are facing the same side up (page 40). Set the fish over the hot coals and grill for a few minutes before turning and grilling on the other side. You want the skin to be crisp and lightly blistered and, using a temperature probe, the fish should be around 55°C (131°F) in the thickest part.

Lift the cage onto a warmed plate and loosely cover with foil, leaving to rest for 10 minutes or so to allow the fish to finish cooking to 60°C (140°F). Slide the pan of butter sauce back over the heat to rewarm for a minute or so if necessary.

To serve, use a fish slice to release the fish from the cage and slide dark-side up onto warmed plates. Use a sharp knife to score down through the centre line from head to tail, then use a fork or clean fingers to peel the skin back a little on each side to reveal the flesh beneath. Pour the hot butter and shrimps over the flesh and serve immediately. Remember to save the fish frames and skin to make stock (page 32).

Serves 2

2 Cornish, or megrim, sole, about
    250–300g (9–10½oz) each
a drizzle of olive oil
1 tbsp flaked sea salt

**For the browned
shrimp butter**

100g (3½oz) butter, chopped into
    1cm (½in) cubes
3 bay leaves
a good pinch of mace, about ¼ tsp
75g (2½oz) cooked peeled
    brown shrimp
flaked sea salt and freshly ground
    black pepper

Turbot with a sherry vinaigrette baste

A whole turbot is a truly special thing. Not even vaguely wallet-friendly, it is widely regarded as one of the best fish you can possibly eat, so something to relish as a once-in-a-while treat for a celebration. Here it is treated in the Basque style, with a simple olive oil and sherry vinegar baste made famous by the restaurant Elkano in northern Spain. Cheekily perhaps, I add a little hint of fennel seed as it feels like such a good flavour to pair with fish.

It goes without saying that you can take a different, less extravagant flatfish and treat it in exactly the same way with equally delicious results. I would eat this with nothing more than new potatoes smothered in butter and a generous fresh green salad.

Rest the turbot on a rack hung over a tray. Slide into the fridge, uncovered, and leave to dry for a good few hours – 12 or even 24 hours wouldn't hurt.

When you are ready to cook, fire up a barbecue or fire pit good and hot, allowing the coals to burn fully. Arrange the embers for direct cooking, so work out how your fish cage sits on the grill bars and use tongs or a fire rake to get the coals underneath. It's much easier to do this before you start cooking the fish and only then realizing your fuel and cage-and-fish arrangement is not aligned. Leave the cage over the fire to heat up. While the fire is heating up, set a small pan on the hob over a medium heat and add the fennel seeds. Toast for a minute or so until they smell fragrant, then tip into a pestle and mortar and grind. Transfer to a small bowl and whisk in the olive oil, sherry vinegar and caster sugar. Season with plenty of black pepper and take to the barbecue with a silicone brush.

Remove the fish from the fridge and brush a little olive oil over both sides, sprinkle with the salt and take to the barbecue. Open the hot fish cage and carefully rest the fish, dark-side down first, and cook for a couple of minutes directly over the hot coals. Turn, baste the top with a little of the vinaigrette and cook for another couple of minutes. Keep turning and basting until the fish reaches 55°C (131°F) when probed in the thickest part; it should take less than 15 minutes in total. Remove the fish cage to a tray, take inside and cover loosely with foil. Leave to rest for about 10 minutes until the temperature is 60°C (140°F).

Use a fish slice to release the fish from the cage and slide onto a warm serving plate. Drizzle with a little more extra virgin olive oil just before serving.

Serves 4

1.4kg (3lb 2oz) turbot
1 heaped tbsp fennel seeds, toasted and coarsely ground
8 tbsp extra virgin olive oil, plus a little for brushing and drizzling
6 tbsp sherry vinegar
a pinch of caster (superfine) sugar
2 tbsp flaked sea salt
freshly ground black pepper

Brill with whipped anchovy butter and caraway carrots

Brill is closely related to turbot and while it used to be a cheaper option, they are pretty evenly matched now, so both are expensive choices to be saved for high days and holidays. The butter here is best whipped fresh just before serving, but you can blanch and marinate the carrots at the same time you set the fish drying, if you want to get ahead.

Several hours before you want to cook, rest the fish on a rack hung over a tray. Slide into the fridge, uncovered, to dry the surface. These fish have pretty thick skins so it will be fine drying for 12 hours, or even overnight. As usual, the drier the skin, the fewer issues you will have with sticking.

Set a large pan of water on the hob and bring to the boil. Cut each carrot into halves or quarters lengthways, depending on how big they are. You want lengths that are about as thick as your thumb. Tip into the pan of boiling water and blanch for 5 minutes, then drain well and put into a shallow bowl where they fit roughly in a single layer. Pour over the olive oil and add the garlic, caraway and a generous grind of salt and pepper. Toss well to coat the carrots in the marinade, then slide the dish into the fridge. The carrots will happily sit for as long as the fish is drying.

When you are ready to cook, fire up the barbecue ready for hot direct grilling (page 31).

While the grill is getting hot, make the anchovy butter. Put the butter, anchovies and garlic in a food processor and whizz until light and creamy. You could use an electric whisk, or even a wooden spoon in a bowl with a lot of elbow grease. Season to taste with black pepper; you probably won't need any salt because of the anchovies. Scoop into a bowl and set aside; it will be fine at room temperature while you cook unless it's a particularly hot day.

When the grill is hot, rest the carrots on the grill bars, lining them up across the bars to stop them falling through, or use a grill tray if you have one. Grill for a few minutes, turning a few times until lightly charred. Remove to a large platter, big enough to fit the fish as well, and slide into a very low oven, set at its lowest setting, to keep warm while you cook the fish.

Serves 4
1.4kg (3lb 2oz) brill
1 tbsp olive oil
2 tbsp flaked sea salt
a handful of dill, chopped,
    to garnish

For the caraway carrots
700g (1lb 9oz) carrots
2 tbsp olive oil
2 garlic cloves, crushed to a paste
1 tbsp caraway seeds, roughly
    crushed
flaked sea salt and freshly ground
    black pepper

For the whipped anchovy butter
100g (3½oz) butter, cut into cubes
8 salted anchovy fillets, roughly
    chopped
2 garlic cloves, crushed to a paste
freshly ground black pepper

Arrange the embers so they are spread out to the same size
as the fish and set a fish cage over the fire to heat up.

Remove the fish from the fridge and rub it all over with the oil.
Sprinkle with the salt on both sides and take to the barbecue.
When the fish cage is hot, rest the fish directly over the heat and
cook for a few minutes each side, maybe 5–6, until the internal
temperature is 55°C (131°F). Remove from the grill and take
inside to rest for a few minutes so the internal temperature
reaches 60°C (140°F). Use a fish slice to ease the skin from the
cage on both sides. Invert onto the warmed platter with the
carrots. Spoon the butter on top, season with salt and pepper and
sprinkle over a little dill. If you are feeling a touch dramatic, you
could pop a glowing ember from the fire on top of the butter so
it sizzles and melts as you take it to the table.

Round white fish

Round fish take a little longer to cook than the flatties as it obviously takes more time for the heat to penetrate the thicker body, but, fish protein being what it is, it's still a relatively quick job when compared to cooking meat. That said, with the following recipes it would always be prudent to leave a good area of the grill fire-free so you have heat control and can slide the fish further away if it looks to be cooking too fast. A temperature probe is such a useful thing here to check how cooking is going, as always with fish cooking you are toeing a fine line between done and overdone.

Unlike flatfish, the round fish are a little easier to turn with a fish slice, or maybe two if it's a biggun, so I tend to prefer to use a hot grill tray rather than a fish cage, although the John Dory is a rather flat fellow so a cage may be easier for that one.

John Dory with cider butter sauce

For a round fish, John Dory is actually not very round at all! A slightly strange, ugly-beautiful kind of fish, it is instantly recognizable by the black spot on its side. Don't be deceived by its skinny nature, there's plenty of firm and very tasty flesh on them bones! Usually a bycatch species (page 10) and while there's not a great deal of scientific evidence to back up population numbers, where they do find their way to the fishmonger's slab, it makes a lot of sense to eat them. If we don't, they would simply go to waste.

The sauce is a take on a Spanish classic hailing from Asturias in the north, where the super-dry 'sidra' is a very big deal. It just happens to be where my dad has lived for decades, and while I cannot bear to drink the stuff, it is mighty fine in cooking. Any dry cider will do if you can't find sidra.

A few hours before you want to cook, lay the fish on a rack over a tray and slide into the fridge, uncovered. This will dry out the skin and help minimize sticking. John Dory, I have discovered, can be a bit of a sticky blighter so it may be good to re-visit page 26 for a bit of a refresh on this perennial fish problem. When you are ready to cook, fire up your barbecue ready for grilling but leaving one area of your grill fire-free so you have heat control (page 31). Set a fish cage or grill tray over the fire to heat up.

While the fire is heating, you can make the sauce, either by setting a flameproof pan over the fire if you have room (putting a pan on top of the heating fish cage is fine) or on the hob inside. Either way, pour in the olive oil and add the onion along with a good pinch of salt, which will help it soften. Cook gently until really soft and lightly caramelized; this will take at least 20 minutes, maybe 30, so don't rush. If you are cooking on the barbecue, you can slide the pan back and forth over the fire to control the heat.

While the onion is cooking, take the tomatoes and grate using a box grater. If you press the cut face firmly to the grating surface, you will be able to neatly remove the flesh from the skin. Discard the skin and scoop the flesh and juice into a bowl.

Serves 2–4, depending on what else you are eating
2 John Dory, about 350–400g (12–14oz) each
1 tbsp olive oil
1 heaped tbsp flaked sea salt
a little flat-leaf parsley, chopped, to garnish

For the cider butter sauce
2 tbsp olive oil
1 large onion, finely chopped
2 large ripe tomatoes, about 200g (7oz), cut in half
3 garlic cloves, crushed to a paste
a pinch of smoked paprika
500ml (17fl oz/2 cups) dry cider
50g (2oz) butter, cut into cubes
flaked sea salt and freshly ground black pepper

Add the garlic to the onion pan and stir briefly before stirring through the tomato pulp, paprika and a grind of black pepper. Cook for about 10 minutes or so until rich and concentrated. Pour in the cider and simmer steadily over a medium–high heat until reduced by half, then drop in the butter cubes and stir until melted. Keep warm while you cook the fish.

Remove the fish from the fridge and drizzle the oil over the top, rubbing it into a thin, even layer. Sprinkle generously with the salt on both sides. Rest the fish on the hot grill tray or in the fish cage and cook for a few minutes on each side. Don't try to turn the fish over too soon; you want it to develop a good crispy skin before you attempt to move it – another way to minimize tearing the skin. Once the fish reaches an internal temperature of 55°C (131°F), remove the tray or cage and take the fish inside to rest for a few minutes to allow the temperature to rise to 60°C (140°F).

To serve, use a fish slice to release the fish from the cage or tray and slide onto warmed plates. Drizzle the warm sauce over the top and sprinkle with a little parsley.

Bass chermoula

Chermoula is a North African herb oil and a traditional accompaniment to fish, a little like pesto or chimichurri in texture but more lemony and a little spicy. I prefer to make it in a large pestle and mortar so it retains some texture, but you can whizz in a processor for a smoother, more hands-off version, or you can finely chop everything and stir in a bowl. I add just a little honey to balance the lemon – it's not traditional but I like it. Taste without, then add if you fancy it. Chermoula basically goes with any fish you like but here I serve it with simple grilled bass, using just a little to baste the fish before grilling and serving the rest as a sauce alongside. I prefer to buy wild bass as a treat when in season, which in the UK is every month except February and March.

A good few hours before you want to cook, rest the bass on a rack over a tray and slide uncovered into the fridge to dry the skin.

If you are making the chermoula by hand in a pestle and mortar, add the toasted cumin first and grind to a coarse powder. Add the garlic, preserved lemon and paprika and season with salt and pepper before pounding together. Add the herbs, lemon juice and oil and pound to mix. Taste and add a little honey, if you like. Scoop most of it into a serving bowl and add just a tablespoon or so into a separate small bowl to baste. Set aside. You can make it a few hours ahead and store in the fridge, if you like.

When you are ready to cook, light the barbecue ready for direct grilling (page 31) and set a grill tray or fish cage over the fire to heat up. When the coals are fully lit, spread them into a thin, even layer the size of your fish.

Take the small bowl of chermoula and brush it over both sides of the fish. Sprinkle with the salt, which will help prevent sticking as well as enhancing flavour.

Take the fish to the grill and rest it on the hot grill tray or in the fish cage. Grill over direct heat for about 5 minutes each side until crispy and cooked to 55°C (131°F). Remove to a plate and rest somewhere warm for a few minutes to allow the temperature to rise to 60°C (140°F).

Use a fish slice to release the fish from the tray or cage and transfer it to a warm serving platter. Serve the rest of the chermoula alongside.

Serves 2, easily doubled

1 x 700g (1lb 9oz) bass,
    preferably wild
1 heaped tbsp flaked sea salt

For the chermoula

1 tbsp cumin seeds, toasted
5 garlic cloves, finely chopped
1 small preserved lemon, peel
    finely chopped, about 1 tbsp
1 tbsp unsmoked paprika
a large bunch of coriander
    (cilantro), about 50g (2oz),
    finely chopped
a good handful of flat-leaf
    parsley, about 25g (¾oz),
    finely chopped
juice of 1 lemon
100ml (3½fl oz/scant ½ cup)
    extra virgin olive oil
1 tbsp honey (optional), to taste
flaked sea salt and freshly ground
    black pepper

Bream with nam jim sauce and coconut rice

As is ubiquitous throughout these pages, this recipe begins with the all-important air drying step, the best way I know to minimize sticking (page 26). The fish, as in so many of the recipes throughout the book, is also sprinkled with a generous quantity of salt flakes, which not only helps prevent sticking, it creates gloriously crisp skin.

Nam jim is a Thai dipping sauce often served with fish, the quantity of which might seem a lot here but, trust me, it is so good – hot, sweet, sour – you will be very glad of extras. Any left over is fantastic as a spiky salad dressing or drizzled over fried eggs or an omelette. I love it so much I could quite happily sip it off a teaspoon.

Place the fish on a rack over a tray and slide into the fridge, uncovered, for a few hours to dry the skin out. This will go a long way to help prevent the fish sticking on cooking.

When you are ready to cook, begin with the rice. Tip it into a saucepan and pour in the coconut cream, giving it a good stir to mix. Add enough cold water to come 1cm (½in) above the level of the rice. Stir through the lemongrass, spring onions and salt. Cover with a lid and set aside to soak for an hour.

Make the nam jim sauce by pounding the chillies and garlic to a crush in a pestle and mortar. Add the sugar, salt and coriander and pound to a coarse paste. Finally pour in the fish sauce and squeeze in the lime juice, pounding together to mix. You can also make this in a mini food processor for a smoother result. Spoon into a small serving dish and set aside.

Once the rice has had its soak, fire up the barbecue ready to cook the fish directly over a hot bed of embers, setting a grill tray or fish cage over the fire to heat up.

Serves 4

4 bream, about 350–380g
  (12–13oz) each
a little vegetable oil, to drizzle
2 heaped tbsp flaked sea salt
2 lemongrass stalks, cut in half
  lengthways
2 spring onions (scallions), cut in
  half lengthways
a few stems of Thai basil, leaves
picked and roughly chopped

For the coconut rice

300g (10½oz/1⅔ cups) Thai
  jasmine rice
180–200ml (6–7fl oz/¾-scant
  1 cup) coconut cream
1 lemongrass stalk, sliced in half
  and bruised with the flat of
  a knife
2 spring onions (scallions), cut
  into 2–3cm (¾–1¼in) chunks
½ tsp flaked sea salt

While the grill is heating, cook the rice. Set the pan over a medium heat on the hob and bring to the boil. Simmer, covered, for 5 minutes, then turn off the heat and leave to rest, still covered, until you are ready to serve. It will take 15 minutes or so to absorb all the liquid but will sit very happily for a good 30–40 minutes.

Once the fire is ready, drizzle a little oil over each fish, rubbing it to an even layer. Sprinkle the salt generously over both sides of the fish and insert a piece of lemongrass and spring onion into the gut cavity of each. Take to the grill and rest on the hot grill tray or in the fish cage. Cook directly over the hot coals for a few minutes on each side, or until the internal temperature is around 55°C (131°F) in the thickest part. Take the fish inside for a few minutes until the temperature increases to 60°C (140°F).

Just before serving, fluff up the rice with a fork and spoon over a serving platter. Ease the fish free from the grill tray or cage and rest on top of the rice. Sprinkle with the basil and drizzle over a little nim jam, serving the rest alongside.

For the nam jim

4–6 bird's-eye chillies, to taste, roughly chopped
5 garlic cloves, roughly chopped
30g (1oz) palm sugar, shaved, or 2 tbsp light soft brown sugar
2 tsp flaked sea salt, about 20g (½oz)
a handful of coriander (cilantro), roughly chopped
4 tbsp fish sauce
juice of 4 limes

Charcoal salt-baked bass and mojo rojo new potatoes

This dish is a little bit of fun but for good reason. Salt baking is an ancient technique for cooking whole fish, where it gets fully enclosed, keeping the moisture locked in so it kind of steam-bakes.

My starting point here was the gorgeous salt-crusted *papas arrugadas* ubiquitous across the Canary Islands that are served with mojo rojo, a spicy red pepper sauce. On a break in Lanzarote, a wild land of black sand and volcanoes, we ate them at every single bar we stopped at. And that was my cue to turning my salt black with charcoal and burying my spuds in with the fish to be dug out like treasure at the table. It won't add anything by way of flavour but it adds a little drama. Cheap table salt is just the thing here as you want to entirely bury the fish in a large quantity, but what you definitely don't want is cheap charcoal. If you are not 100% sure of your charcoal source – it should smell of nothing, remember page 12? – then just leave it out.

Tip the potatoes into a pan and cover well with cold water. Set on the hob, bring up to the boil and cook until tender, around 15 minutes or so depending on their size. Drain well, toss in a little olive oil and set aside.

Meanwhile, fire up the barbecue to create an oven-like indirect heat, with two strips of fire down either side and a generous fire-free zone in the middle where you can bake the fish. Adjust your air vents – you are aiming for a hot oven-like temperature of around 220°C (428°F).

Tip the salt into a mixing bowl. If you are using charcoal, grind it to a powder – I use a small food processor that gets well rinsed and then goes through the dishwasher and comes out sparkling. You could use a pestle and mortar or put it in a plastic bag and bang it with a rolling pin! Either way, tip the powder into the salt, then stir through the measured water until you have a sandy paste.

Take a flameproof pan and spoon about one-third of the salt mix into the base. Drizzle a little oil on the fish and rub all over. Tuck the thyme and lemon slices in the gut cavity. Rest the fish in the pan and tuck the cooked potatoes all around. Scoop the rest of the salt mix over the top and use your hands to press it around so it covers the fish and potatoes as best you can. It doesn't matter if the head and tails are exposed a little but make sure the fish bodies and potatoes are all covered.

Serves 4

1kg (2lb 4oz) small new potatoes, scrubbed
olive oil, to drizzle
3kg (6lb 10oz) fine table salt
a handful of pure charcoal lumps (optional, see intro)
500ml (17fl oz/2 cups) cold water
2 x 600g (1lb 5oz) wild bass, gutted
a good handful of thyme sprigs
1 lemon, sliced

Place the pan in the centre of the barbecue between the two fires and shut the lid. Bake for around 30 minutes until the salt is hard. A probe inserted through the salt deep into the fish should read 60°C (140°F).

While the fish is cooking, make the mojo rojo, which you can do in a food processor or liquidizer or with a stick blender in a deep jug. Either way, you want to blitz the peppers raw with the garlic, olive oil, vinegar, cumin, paprika and chilli. Season with plenty of pepper but go easy on the salt – you probably won't need any because of the salt round the fish. Scoop into a bowl.

To serve, put the pan on a board in the centre of the table and use a knife to slice away the salt layer to reveal the fish below; it should come away in big lumps. Remove the skin, taking care not to let the salt fall onto the flesh otherwise it will be overly salty, and use a palette knife to fillet the fish from the bone. Dig around to find the potatoes and serve with the mojo rojo alongside.

For the mojo rojo
2 Romano peppers, deseeded
    and roughly chopped
3 fat garlic cloves
5 tbsp extra virgin olive oil
2 tbsp red wine vinegar
1 tsp cumin seeds, toasted
    and ground
1 tsp smoked paprika
a pinch of dried chilli (hot
    pepper) flakes, to taste
flaked sea salt and freshly ground
    black pepper

Grilled gurnard with peperonata

Gurnard are weirdly beautiful fish with firm, tasty flesh and a sort of triangular-shaped body, meaning you get three sides to grill, which does mean an extra side to stick and makes for a slightly awkward shape to cook. My best advice? Go with the flow, do your best with my anti-sticking tips on page 26 and, once cooked, just get stuck in with forks to pull off the big juicy flakes as you eat. Gurnard are big-headed fish with strong bones that would be a shame to waste so keep the frames post eating to make some excellent stock (page 32).

The Italian peperonata is rather unauthentic with the addition of Kalamata olives, anchovies and oregano, like the dish went on a Greek beach holiday, but I think it's the essence of a perfect fish accompaniment. This is sunshine food ideal for summer high days, and also to add cheer on the low days that are not as radiant as you would like. No coincidence that the other gurnard recipe in this book (page 95) also relies heavily on ripe tomatoes – they are just a perfect match.

A few hours (up to 12 will be fine) before you want to cook, rest the gurnard on a rack over a tray and slide into the fridge to dry the skin.

When you are ready to cook, fire up the barbecue with the coals on one half, so you can cook both directly and indirectly (page 31). Set a grill tray over the fire to heat up.

To make the peperonata, tip the peppers and onions into a roasting pan and drizzle over the olive oil, tossing to mix. Set the pan onto the grill bars over the fire (it's fine to sit it on top of the heating grill tray) and shut the lid. Cook for 15 minutes or so, giving the vegetables time to colour a little at the edges, then slide the pan further from the fire and stir through the tomatoes, olives, anchovies, garlic, most of the oregano and a good grind of pepper. Shut the lid so they can continue cooking over the indirect heat and leave for another 20 minutes or so until the tomatoes are just collapsing. Remove and cover with foil to keep warm while you cook the gurnard.

Remove the gurnard from the fridge, brush all over with the oil, then sprinkle generously with the salt and take to the barbecue.

Rest the fish on the hot grill tray over the fire, belly-side down. Cook for a few minutes before using a fish slice to ease the skin from the tray and turn the fish onto one side. If it's a little stuck, leave it for another minute before trying again. Cook for another

Serves 2, generously

700–750g (1lb 9oz–1lb 10oz) red gurnard, gutted through the belly
1 tbsp olive oil
1 heaped tbsp flaked sea salt

For the peperonata

2 red or orange peppers, chopped into 3cm (1¼in) pieces
2 red onions, chopped
4 tbsp olive oil
300g (10½oz) cherry tomatoes, halved
a good handful of pitted Kalamata olives, chopped
30g (1oz) anchovy fillets, roughly chopped
3 garlic cloves, sliced
a bunch of oregano, leaves picked, about 15g (½oz)
freshly ground black pepper

few minutes before turning onto the other side and repeating. Once the fish is crispy skinned all over, check the temperature – it should be 55°C (131°F) or so in the deepest part. If it's not quite there, slide the tray away from the fire, shut the lid and leave for a few minutes before checking again. Once it's at temperature, remove the cover and rest for a few minutes.

While the gurnard is resting, return the peperonata to the barbecue and shut the lid to let it warm a little.

Once the fish is 60°C (140°F) in the centre, remove the peperonata from the grill, and uncover. Use a couple of fish slices to carefully lift the gurnard from the grill tray, set it on top of the peperonata and sprinkle with the remaining oregano.

Red mullet, feta, garlic and lemon new potatoes

This is easy sunshine fish on the grill: bright, colourful, citrussy and inspired by the kind of thing I want to eat on holiday, or indeed when I am wishing I was on holiday! Red mullet is a brilliant fish to grill; with a higher fat content than other white fish they hold together well. They are widespread in the north Atlantic and the Mediterranean and currently a sustainable choice for a British consumer as they are frequent summer visitors around Cornwall. Head back to page 8 for the lowdown on how I choose the fish I buy. Mackerel would be a great alternative in the recipe.

A few hours, perhaps 3–4, before you want to cook, rest the mullet on a rack over a tray and slide into the fridge to air dry. When you are ready to cook, fire up your barbecue ready for direct and indirect grilling – so with a layer of hot coals on one side, and no coals on the other side (page 31). Set a perforated grill tray over the fire to get hot.

Tip the potato slices into a flameproof baking pan and tuck in the garlic and lemon wedges, giving them a squeeze to release some of their juice. Sprinkle with the oregano and season well with salt and pepper. Drizzle the olive oil over the top and toss to mix.

Set the pan on the grill bars on top of the grill tray and cook with the lid down for around an hour until soft and slightly crispy in places. You will need to stir the potatoes from time to time, sliding the tray off the heat a little if they are catching and sliding it closer if you want more crispiness.

Once the spuds are done, remove the pan but leave the hot grill tray in place. Sprinkle the potatoes with the feta and cover snugly with foil, then set aside in the kitchen to keep warm.

Remove the fish from the fridge and drizzle with the oil, rubbing it in all over. Sprinkle generously with the salt and take to the barbecue. Rest on the hot grill tray over the fire. Cook for about 8–10 minutes, using a fish slice to turn over once during cooking. When the skin is super-crisp and the temperature reads 55°C (131°F) or so when probed in the deepest part, transfer to a pan and take inside.

Rest the fish over the potatoes and re-cover with foil, leaving to rest for a few minutes so the fish temperature rises to 60°C (140°F) or so. To serve, squeeze over the lemon wedges, drizzle generously with extra virgin olive oil and scatter on the parsley.

Serves 4

4 red mullet, about 225g
(8oz) each
1 tbsp olive oil
2 tbsp flaked sea salt

For the potatoes

1kg (2lb 4oz) new potatoes,
sliced in 5mm (¼in) discs
1 bulb of garlic, cloves whole,
peeled
1 lemon, cut into 8 wedges
1 tbsp dried oregano
2 tbsp olive oil
200g (7oz) feta, crumbled
flaked sea salt and freshly ground
black pepper

To serve

1 lemon, cut into wedges
extra virgin olive oil
a good handful of flat-leaf
parsley, chopped

Round oily fish

If anything smells of holidays it's grilling anchovies, sardines and mackerel, some of the best tasting and healthiest fish we can eat. Just one whiff and I'm back on the shores of the Med and it's no coincidence that these oily round fish are grilled so much in southern Europe. They just respond so well to the direct heat of the fire with a higher fat content than white fish helping to keep the flesh succulent.

All the usual same rules apply – dry skin, high heat, quick cooking – but they are more forgiving than their less oily cousins. Yes, they will possibly still catch a little and the skin may tear – they are fairly thin-skinned when compared to something like a flatfish – but the eating enjoyment certainly won't be diminished; just make sure you scrape up and enjoy the crispy bits that may be stuck to the tray.

Also, as shoaling species, they can be found in abundance at certain times of year so these round oily fish can be some of most sustainable fish available. A gentle reminder then that the concept of 'good fish' (see page 8) means we always need to be guided by the seasonality of the fish we buy. Thanks to global warming, both seasons and fish are fluctuating more than ever, so we need to be in tune with the picture as it is currently – which why there are no season-specific charts in this book. Find suppliers you trust and be guided by both them and the latest science. Head to page 266 for resources to help.

Sardines with tomato dressing

I cook these – always super-fresh, whole and ungutted – with a simple dressing poured as soon as they hit the grill. This is cooking fish over fire at its simplest but if you are a little squeamish about the ungutted nature of these, you can obviously either gut them yourself or ask your fishmonger to do it for you. Sardines have a thin skin and can be prone to sticking a little. As usual, follow the tips on page 26 to minimize this problem but don't worry about it too much. Little sticky, slightly burnt bits kind of add to this experience. By the way, don't even think about eating these with a knife and fork – that's way too fiddly and unsatisfying. Just pick them up with your fingers and nibble round the frame like a cartoon cat, saving the fork only to scoop on bits of tomato and dressing.

Note: if you have neither a fish cage nor grill tray you can thread onto skewers and cook kebab-style, see the Fish on a Stick chapter (page 112) for visual inspiration.

When you get the sardines home, take them out of their packaging and line up on a rack hung over a tray. Slide into the fridge and leave to dry the skin for up to 12 hours.

When you are ready to cook, get your dressing ready before you even think about grilling the fish, as you want to tuck in to eat these as soon as they come off the barbecue.

Use a sharp knife to score round the middle of each tomato and transfer to a heatproof bowl. Boil a kettle of water, then pour it over the tomatoes and leave for a minute. Drain the water away and, once the tomatoes are cool enough to handle, peel away and discard the skin. Finely dice the flesh and scoop into a bowl. Pour over the extra virgin olive oil, add the lemon zest and juice, parsley and garlic and season with salt and pepper. Use a fork to whisk together until combined. Set aside at room temperature.

When you are ready to cook, fire up your grill for direct hot cooking, allowing the coals to cook down to embers (page 31) and set a grill tray or fish cage over the fire the get hot. Once hot, drizzle a little oil all over the sardines and sprinkle generously with the salt. Transfer to the hot grill tray or fish cage and set back over the direct heat. Cook for a couple of minutes on each side until lightly charred all over.

Transfer to a serving plate, using a fish slice to scrape over any little stuck bits on top of the fish (too good to waste!). Pour over the dressing and tuck right in.

Serves 4

1kg (2lb 4oz) whole sardines
a drizzle of olive oil
2 tbsp flaked sea salt

For the dressing

3 large ripe vine tomatoes
100ml (3½fl oz/scant ½ cup)
    extra virgin olive oil
1 lemon, zest and juice
a loose handful of flat-leaf parsley,
    about 15g (¾oz), chopped
2 garlic cloves, finely chopped
flaked sea salt and freshly ground
    black pepper

Devilled mackerel

Devilled refers to the spiciness of the marinade, although if you tone down the cayenne it's a much less intense affair. The simplicity here is good, and I would serve these with no more than good bread and butter, a little green salad and a squeeze of lemon juice.

A word of warning: the marinade here is quite thick and the fish's skin quite shiny, so you may get annoyed that it's not sticking well. Just do your best and make sure to rub plenty of the marinade inside the gut cavity and then, over a long marinating time, the flavours will work their magic. Due to the mustard, these fish are even more prone to sticking than normal, so if you have some large skewers you can thread them up – as in the picture – and hang them between bricks over the fire.

About 6–12 hours before you want to cook, make the marinade by mixing together the olive oil, both mustards, the garlic, paprika, ginger and cayenne pepper. Season well with salt and pepper.

Rest the mackerel in a dish or roasting pan in a single, snug layer and scoop on the marinade. Use your hands, with gloves if you are sensitive to chilli, and rub well all over, including inside the gut cavity. Slide into the fridge and leave to marinate for a good few hours – overnight if you have time.

When you are ready to cook, fire up the barbecue ready for direct grilling, allowing the coals to burn fully hot before you cook. If you are not cooking on skewers hung over the fire, set a fish cage or grill tray over the fire to heat up.

When the fire is ready to cook on (see page 31 for fire tips), cook the mackerel for a few minutes each side until the outside is crisp and lightly charred and the internal temperature is 60°C (140°F). Serve hot from the fire.

Serves 4

2 tbsp olive oil
3 tbsp whole grain mustard
3 tbsp English mustard powder
3 garlic cloves, crushed to a paste
1 tbsp smoked paprika
2 tsp ground ginger
2 tsp cayenne pepper, or to taste
4 mackerel, about 300g (10½oz)
    each, gutted
flaked sea salt and freshly ground
    black pepper

Mackerel 'canoe' stuffed with spiced currant rice, dill oil and pistachio

A fish stuffed with a lovely Middle Eastern inspired spicy rice. Canoe stuffing, or 'pocket' stuffing as I think of it, is a different way to butcher a fish. It means you get a more generous pocket to stuff tasty things in than you could if you just used the gut cavity. Head back to page 21 if you want to try to canoe-bone your mackerel, otherwise ask your fishmonger nicely to do it for you. It's really not hard – you are simply removing the backbone through the top rather than the bottom – and if it's not perfect it won't matter a jot.

You could take your rice in a different direction if you fancied – cumin and coriander seed with fresh coriander oil would be lovely.

Set the mackerel skin-side up, so pocket-side down, on a rack over a tray and slide into the fridge to dry out the skin for a few hours.

When you are ready to cook, fire up the barbecue ready for direct grilling but as usual leaving a fire-free zone for heat control (page 31). Set a grill tray over the fire as it heats to get hot.

Start the filling by setting a pan over a medium heat, either on the barbecue as the charcoal is heating or inside on the hob. Pour in the olive oil, add the onion and fry for a good 20 minutes until soft and lightly caramelized. Once the onion is soft, reduce the heat to low and add the garlic, currants, allspice, cinnamon and chilli. Season to taste with salt and pepper.

While the onion is cooking, make the dill oil by mixing together the finely chopped dill with the oil and a generous grind of salt and pepper. Set aside.

Cook the rice in boiling water until just tender, drain well and rinse under cold water to separate the grains. Tip into the onion mixture and stir together over a low heat for a couple of minutes until hot.

Remove the mackerel from the fridge and drizzle a little olive oil over the skin. Sprinkle the skin side generously with the salt and rub in.

Serves 2

2 mackerel, canoe boned, about
    300g (10½oz) each
a drizzle of olive oil
1 tbsp flaked sea salt

For the filling

3 tbsp olive oil
1 red onion, finely chopped
3 garlic cloves, crushed to a paste
50g (2oz) currants
1 heaped tsp ground allspice
1 heaped tsp ground cinnamon
½–1 tsp dried chilli (hot pepper)
    flakes, to taste
100g (3½oz/heaped ½ cup) white
    rice
flaked sea salt and freshly ground
    black pepper

For the dill oil

15g (½oz) dill, finely chopped
75ml (5 tbsp) olive oil

To garnish

50g (2oz/⅓ cup) shelled pistachios,
    toasted and chopped
a little extra dill, roughly chopped

You also need a few metal skewers

Turn over so the pocket is facing upwards. Divide the hot filling into the cavity and push it well in. The fish will splay out (looking like a fat open canoe, hence the name) so poke a few skewers through to secure it as best you can. Take the tray to the barbecue along with a fish slice.

Use the fish slice to help you slide the mackerel, one at a time, onto the hot grill tray over the fire. Cook over the hot embers until the skin is crispy and the fish is cooked – a probe should read 60°C (140°F) in the deepest part of the fish.

To serve, use the fish slice to help ease the fish skin from the tray and slide onto plates. Drizzle over the dill oil, then scatter on the pistachios and sprinkle over the extra dill.

Chapter 2:
Bits of fish

If you don't have a whole fish, you have bits of fish, so in this chapter you will find the steaks, fillets and whole sides. A few of these recipes are super-simple, even more so if you bypass the fish prep and get your fishmonger to do all the hard work. And why not? They are no doubt the more skilled operators here. Some recipes are rather more involved because often the actual fish element is pretty speedy, and while you can't cook fish on the rising heat of a young fire (see page 31), you can maximize the heat potential in the coals by cooking something else beforehand.

A grill tray is a better option in these recipes than it would be for a whole large fish, but you may find a fish cage easier to turn several fillets over in one fell swoop. See page 24 for kit chat. Either way, you need to ensure it is really very hot before it meets the fish – that is one of the most useful and easy tips I can give you in this whole book. Head back to page 26 for solving the sticky fish problem.

Fish weights

One little annoying thing, fish fillets do have a tendency to curl up when they hit the heat, meaning you lose your chance for the crispiest skin, and crisp skin is invariably the end goal. The short protein blocks are stacked like bricks, if you remember (page 26), and the connective tissues between each block cooks very fast, much faster than in meat, so the fillet will misshape almost as soon as it hits the heat. The best thing to do is start by cooking skin-side down and as soon as the fillet hits the hot surface put some sort of weight onto it. You can buy dedicated fish weights designed for this exact purpose, but they can be pretty spendy. I don't have one and tend to just grab a heavyweight frying pan, lightly oiled on the base so it doesn't stick to the fish, and whack that onto the fillets. Does the job nicely.

Tuna, good and bad

Man, I just love, love, love fresh tuna, and so it seems does everyone else. Tuna is one of the 'big 5' fish I mention on page 10, the ones we turn to time and time again. I think we love it for the universal boneless appeal of its fillets as well as its meaty steak-like texture. Cooked simply on a sizzling hot grill (preferably in the sunshine with friends and wine), I think it is one of life's great pleasures. But – there's always a but – in terms of sustainability there is definitely 'bad' tuna and 'good' tuna, and in the UK even the 'good' tuna mostly comes from quite a long way away, so for me, as much as I love it, it's an occasional treat in our house – like avocados and perfectly ripe pineapples.

An apex predator, like a lion or a cheetah, these guys are at the top of their food chain, which in broad ecological terms means if we eat them all, then the entire system below them fails. We therefore need to fish them with care to ensure the health of the rest of the oceans. In any ecosystem, on land or sea, when you protect the apex predator you look after the whole system in its entirety.

Just like good steak, good tuna is, or should be, a once-in-a-while treat. Currently, at the time of writing, I believe albacore tuna caught by certified fleets with a pole-and-line method in the North Atlantic and South Pacific is the best choice and has Marine Stewardship Council status. Certainly albacore tuna is my favourite for flavour and texture. Skipjack and Yellowfin tuna, again caught by pole and line in certain places, is also a good choice. As ever, these things change constantly so check out current scientific advice (see page 266). What is very clear is that pole and line is the only way to sustainably fish for tuna.

Miso and sesame tuna steaks with wasabi ginger mayo

Treat a tuna steak like a beef steak – you can eat it how you like! My personal preference is not too rare. I really like beef steaks rare but I prefer tuna not so rare; medium is more my bag, but this is your dinner, so you get to choose. Do use a temperature probe if you have one. With fish, you are always treading a fine line between done and overdone because of the structure of fish proteins (I refer you back to page 26). A medium tuna steak will be cooked at around 50°C (122°F) so go a few degrees either side as is your preference.

Serve with sticky sushi rice or green salad or maybe even both. Other good things to eat with a tuna steak are garlic mayo or flavoured herb butters, recipes for which are scattered through the book.

About an hour before you want to cook, marinate the tuna. Pour the soy into a small bowl and add the miso and a generous grind of black pepper, stirring together to make a smooth, thin paste. Rest the tuna on a plate in a snug single layer, pour the marinade over and rub in all over. Slide into the fridge for an hour or so.

Meanwhile, take a small bowl and stir together the mayonnaise, wasabi to taste, pickled ginger, garlic and a generous grind of black pepper. Set aside in the fridge.

When you are ready to cook, fire up the barbecue ready for hot direct grilling, letting the coals cook to a bed of embers and setting a grill tray or fish cage over the fire to heat up.

When the barbecue is hot and good to go, sprinkle the sesame seeds over a plate in a shallow layer. Take the tuna steaks and press one side then the other into the seeds, then roll along the edge too. Take to the barbecue along with the sesame oil.

Drizzle a little sesame oil over the uppermost side of each steak, then lift and rest oil-side down on the hot grill tray. Drizzle a little more oil over the top side. Cook for a minute or so until the white sesame seeds are golden, then use a fish slice to flip over and cook the other side for another minute. Slide the tray off the heat and use a temperature probe to gauge doneness: around 50°C (122°F) will give you a medium steak, a few degrees less will be rarer, a few more will be well done.

Serves 2

2 tbsp soy sauce
1 tbsp miso paste
2 x 175–200g (6–7oz) tuna steaks
60g (2oz) sesame seeds (a mix of black and white if you can get them, or just white)
1 tbsp toasted sesame oil

For the wasabi ginger mayo

4 tbsp mayonnaise
1–2 tbsp wasabi paste, to taste
1–2 tbsp pickled ginger, to taste, chopped
1 garlic clove, crushed to a paste
freshly ground black pepper

Whiting with lemongrass and lime leaf butter

Whiting are smaller relatives of cod and haddock, low-fat, white-fleshed fish that are prone to sticking. They do, however, have good thick skins, so in this recipe the whole fish fillets, after drying, are cooked just on the skin side until the skin is super-crispy and tasty and the flesh is just cooked through. The butter sauce is simple but insanely good, slightly browned from the heat and flavoured with lemongrass and lime leaves, but any of the flavoured butters in the book would work well with whiting.

Begin by resting the fillets, skin-side up, on a rack hung over a tray. Slide into the fridge and leave to dry for 6 hours or so.

When you are ready to cook, fire up the barbecue ready for direct grilling. You won't need much fuel as the thin fillets are quick to cook. Set a grill tray over the fire and leave to get hot.

Remove the tough outer leaves from the lemongrass and very finely chop the rest of the stem. Remove the central rib from the lime leaves and very finely chop the rest of the leaves.

Set a small pan over the fire and drop in the butter, allowing it to melt. It's fine to sit the pan on top of the heating grill tray. Add the chopped lemongrass and lime leaves and season with salt and pepper. Swirl the pan over the heat until the butter has very lightly browned, then slide off the heat to keep warm.

Remove the fish from the fridge and drizzle with the olive oil, rubbing it over into a thin, even layer. Sprinkle well with the salt. The salt also helps with sticking as it forms a slightly protective barrier between skin and grill tray. Lightly oil the underside of your fish weight or pan, just something heavy you can use to stop them curling up (page 75).

Rest the fillets skin-side down onto the hot grill tray and quickly set the oiled weight or pan on top.

Grill over a high heat for just 3 minutes or so until the flesh is opaque and flaky and the skin is super-crisp. To serve, use a fish slice to tease the fillets off the grill tray surface. Rest skin-side up on a warmed plate and pour over the butter.

Serves 2

2 whiting fillets, about 200g
(7oz) each
1 tbsp olive oil
2 tsp flaked sea salt

For the butter

1 lemongrass stalk
4 double-lobed fresh lime leaves
75g (2½oz) butter
flaked sea salt and freshly ground
black pepper

Nori-wrapped cod with sesame rice cakes and soy dipping sauce

Cod had a dreadful sustainability question mark over it for some time but currently, thanks to careful fisheries management, it is now doing rather well. Situations change every season, and I refer you back to page 10 for advice on choosing your fish. Cod stocks are currently strong, particularly in Iceland and the north-east Atlantic, on a par with haddock, which would be a very good alternative fish here.

You can get the rice cakes made well ahead of time but you need to prep the fish within 30 minutes of cooking as the nori starts to soften too much otherwise.

Nori seaweed sheets are really easy to find in supermarkets these days but there is a growing British seaweed industry so it's worth keeping an eye out for more local seaweeds. As usual, the internet is your friend for sourcing ingredients – see pages 266–269 for suppliers. Togarashi is a lovely Japanese spice mix that adds a little chilli hit as a garnish, but feel free to use a sprinkle of dried chilli (hot pepper) flakes or splash of any hot sauce, if you prefer.

Tip the rice into a pan and add the boiling water. Cover with a tight-fitting lid or snugly wrapped piece of foil. Simmer gently for 15 minutes, then turn off the heat but leave covered and allow to rest for 10 minutes. Stir through the sesame oil, sesame seeds and a generous seasoning of salt and pepper. Leave to one side until cool enough to shape with your hands, then crack in the eggs and stir well. Divide into 12 satsuma-sized balls, pressing them firmly together between your palms to stick the grains together. Damp hands will help prevent the mixture from sticking too much. Compress the balls into flat fritters about 1cm (½in) thick and line up on a lightly oiled plate. Cover and slide into the fridge to chill until you are ready to cook. They will keep happily in the fridge for 24 hours if you want to get ahead.

At the same time, pour the soy sauce into a small pan and set over a medium heat on the hob. Add the ginger, garlic and a generous grind of black pepper. Bring to the boil, then simmer for 5 minutes. Turn off the heat, pour into a bowl and set aside for serving. You can also chill in the fridge for a day or so if you want to get ahead.

When you are ready to cook, fire up the barbecue ready for direct grilling.

Serves 4
8 sheets dried nori
a little sesame oil, to brush
700g (1lb 9oz) chunky, skinless cod fillets, cut into 4

For the sesame rice cakes
350g (12oz/1¾ cups) sushi rice
500ml (17fl oz/2 cups) boiling water
3 tbsp toasted sesame oil
3 tbsp sesame seeds, toasted for a minute in a dry pan
2 eggs
vegetable oil, for shallow frying
flaked sea salt and freshly ground black pepper

For the soy dipping sauce
100ml (3½fl oz/scant ½ cup) soy sauce
25g (¾oz) ginger root, sliced into thin matchsticks
2 garlic cloves, thinly sliced

Take a sheet of nori and brush lightly on one side with sesame oil, then rest another sheet on top to form a double layer and brush again. Place a piece of cod in the centre and fold the nori up and over to make a neat parcel, securing each one with a small metal skewer, if you have some – like wrapping a little fishy present – then rest it seam-side down on a plate. If your fish fillets are thin, you can cut them into pieces and stack them up before wrapping together. Repeat with the rest of the nori and cod to give to 4 parcels in total. Brush with just a little more sesame oil and set aside while you cook the rice cakes.

Set a large flameproof frying pan over the fire and pour in a generous glug of vegetable oil to form a shallow layer about 2mm deep. Leave for a few minutes to get really hot – leaving the barbecue lid off at this point will allow oxygen to flow through the fire and keep the heat high (page 28).

Take the rice cakes from the fridge and place in the hot oil, frying for about 6–7 minutes on each side until lightly golden. Remove to an ovenproof dish lined with a few sheets of paper towel and keep warm – if you have fire-free space to one edge of your barbecue they will rest there happily while you cook the fish. You could, of course, fry the rice cakes on the hob inside, but if you have a lit fire, why not stay outside?

Give the grill bars a quick scrub with a stiff wire brush to make sure they are really clean. Rest the wrapped and oiled fish parcels onto the grill bars directly over the fire, seam-side down first so they don't unravel. Cook for a few minutes on each side until the temperature in the centre of the fish is 60°C (140°F) when probed.

Serve the fish with the rice cakes and the dipping sauce alongside, along with carrot and cucumber slivers for added crunch. Finish with a sprinkle of togarashi to add a little heat, if you like.

To serve
slivers of carrot and cucumber
togarashi seasoning (optional)

Trout sides stuffed with spiced onions, coconut and cardamon sauce

A recipe using large, salmon-sized trout, using two fillets stuffed in between with sweet spiced onions. What you get is a 'joint' of trout suitable for carving at the table, Sunday-lunch style. Head on back to page 11 for the story on why I always, now I know, buy trout over salmon.

Buying two large fillets for this recipe is a little spendy but, as a celebratory dish, not much more than a good joint of meat for a roast would cost you. You could, of course, make smaller individual portions by stuffing, tying and grilling small trout fillets. They would take less time to cook. I would serve this with a big bowl of steamed rice and greens stir-fried in butter.

A few hours, or up to 12, before you want to cook, take the trout fillets and rest skin-side up on a rack hung over a tray. Slide into the fridge and leave to dry the skin.

Fire up the barbecue ready for direct and indirect grilling (page 31).

Once the fish has finished drying, set a large frying pan over the fire and tip in the cumin and coriander seeds and the chilli flakes. Toast for a couple of minutes, then transfer to a spice mill or pestle and mortar and grind to a coarse powder.

Slide the pan further away from the fire for a lower heat and add the butter. Once it has melted, add the onions and ground spices, along with the onion seeds and cinnamon. Season with salt and pepper and cook gently for a generous 40 minutes, stirring every now and then, until the onions are soft and melting. Stir through the curry leaves for the last 10 minutes of cooking. Remove from the heat and set aside. You can also do this on the hob inside, if you prefer, in which case don't light the barbecue until the onions are getting towards being ready.

Set a grill cage over the fire to get hot.

Serves 6

2 x 600–700g (1lb 5oz–1lb 9oz) trout sides
1 tbsp cumin seeds
1 tbsp coriander seeds
½–1 tsp dried chilli (hot pepper) flakes, to taste
50g (2oz) butter
4–5 red onions, sliced, about 500–600g (1lb 2oz–1lb 5oz)
1 tbsp black onion seeds
1 tsp ground cinnamon
a few stems of fresh curry leaves
1 tbsp olive oil
flaked sea salt and freshly ground black pepper

While the cage is heating, make the sauce. You can do this on the hob or set a pan over the fire (it's fine to set the pan on top of the heating fish cage). Either way, pour the coconut milk into a small, heavy-based pan and add the garlic, turmeric, cardamom seeds and chilli flakes, stirring over a medium heat. Bring up to a simmer, then add the lime juice, brown sugar and coriander, along with a good seasoning of salt and pepper. Allow to bubble for 10 minutes or so, then remove from the heat and set aside for the flavours to infuse.

Remove the fish from the fridge, turning one fillet so it is skin-side down. Scoop the warm onion on top, spreading it out to form an even layer, then rest the other fillet on top, lining it up with the bottom fillet to completely enclose the onions. Take 5–6 lengths of butcher's twine and tie around at intervals to secure the fish together snugly – enlist help from an extra pair of hands to get the knots good and tight as it's a little fiddly on your own.

Brush the olive oil all over, then sprinkle with 2 tablespoons of sea salt flakes. Make sure the fish cage is super-hot, then rest the oiled fish into it. Set on the grill bars over the embers and cook – turning the fish cage over a few times to ensure the fish skin is crisping evenly (page 27) until a thermometer reads 55°C (131°F) in the thickest part.

Set the fish cage onto a tray and take inside to rest for 10 minutes or so to allow the internal temperature to rise to 60°C (140°F). While the fish is resting, warm the sauce through.

Use a palette knife to gently ease the skin from the fish cage and turn out onto a warm platter. Drizzle over a little of the sauce, serving the rest in a small jug alongside. Sprinkle with a little coriander and chopped chilli. Carve into slices to serve.

For the sauce

1 x 400g (14oz) can of coconut milk
3 garlic cloves, crushed to a paste
25g (¾oz) fresh turmeric root, grated
8 cardamon pods, seeds picked and ground
a pinch of dried chilli (hot pepper) flakes, to taste
juice of 1 lime
1 tsp brown sugar
a small handful of coriander (cilantro), chopped, plus extra to garnish
red chillies, to garnish

To serve

rice and greens

Pepes ikan

Pepes is the Indonesian method of wrapping food in banana leaves before grilling, a technique very often used for fish, or ikan in Indonesian. It's unlikely you'll find banana leaves in your local supermarket but you should easily pick them up in Asian food shops, often in the freezer. Just defrost for a little while before heating as described here to make them flexible. If you can't find them, you can use sheets of damp baking parchment, but the leaves do impart a slightly tannic flavour that is delicious. Just as on the previous recipe, if you have thinner fillets just stack them up to make a nice chunky layer.

This fish goes brilliantly with Coconut rice (page 58).

Put the garlic, shallots, tomatoes, ginger, lemongrass, nuts, tamarind, turmeric, chilli flakes and shrimp paste in a mini food processor. Blitz to a paste. You can also use a stick blender and a deep jug or finely chop and pound everything together in a pestle and mortar for a chunkier result. You can make the paste up to 24 hours ahead if you want to.

Take the banana leaves and use scissors to snip off the stiff central ridge if it is there, otherwise it will prevent your leaves from folding neatly. Using tongs, one leaf at a time, hold just above a gas flame for a few seconds to soften, moving the leaf around constantly until you feel it becoming more floppy and flexible. Repeat with the other leaves. If you happen to already have the barbecue lit, you can obviously bypass the gas!

Lay a piece of fish in the centre of each piece of leaf and spoon the spice paste on top, spreading it all over both sides of the fish. Fold up the sides of the banana leaves and roll up snugly into parcels so the fish is completely wrapped. Secure the edges shut with cocktail sticks (toothpicks) or small skewers and slide into the fridge on a plate to marinate for 30–60 minutes. You can also tie the parcels up with strips of banana leaf if you have spare, or even lengths of string would be fine.

Light the barbecue ready for direct grilling. When the embers are hot, lay the banana leaf parcels over the fire and cook for a few minutes, turning regularly until the leaves are lightly charred. Use a temperature probe to check the fish for doneness; you want it to be 60°C (140°F) in the thickest part.

Serve the parcels with a wedge of lime to squeeze over the fish once unwrapped.

Makes 4

For the spice paste
3 garlic cloves, roughly chopped
2 banana shallots, roughly chopped
2 ripe tomatoes, about 100g (3½oz), roughly chopped
25g (¾oz) ginger root, roughly chopped
1 lemongrass stalk, roughly chopped
40g (½oz/¼ cup) candlenuts or macadamia nuts, toasted
1 tbsp tamarind paste or 1 tsp concentrated tamarind
1 tsp ground turmeric
½–1 tsp dried chilli (hot pepper) flakes, to taste
½ tsp shrimp paste
4 large pieces banana leaf, about 30–35cm (12–14in) lengths (defrosted if frozen)
700g (1lb 9oz) chunky white skinless fish fillets, cut into 4 even pieces (cod, haddock, pollack, ling)

To serve
2 limes, cut into wedges

Bass fillets with walnut crumbs with watercress, tomato and balsamic salad

When I was young, Mum often used to make us a grilled plaice dish with a herby breadcrumb and cheese topping. The fish got no more cooking than it took to crisp up the crumbs under an overhead grill (broiler). That memory was my starting point for this recipe, but I flipped the heat to come from below to give me crisp skin and a crumbly, nutty top – a simple, quick supper made for those summer nights when you just want to sit, eat and chat in the garden. Both the oil and balsamic drizzle over salad and fish is an important layer of flavour so do use the best you can get.

Rest the fish, skin-side up, on a rack over a tray and slide into the fridge uncovered for a few hours to dry the surface.

When you are ready to cook, light the barbecue ready for direct grilling, spreading the embers out to a thin layer. The bass will cook quickly so you won't need too much charcoal.

As the barbecue heats up, set a small flameproof pan over the fire and tip in the walnuts. Leave for a few minutes to toast a few shades darker and until lightly charred in places. Remove the pan and set a grill tray over the fire to heat up.

Scoop the parsley into a small food processor and add the garlic cloves, toasted walnuts and a grind of salt and pepper. Blitz until finely chopped then transfer to a small bowl ready to take to the barbecue. You can also finely chop everything by hand or pound in a pestle and mortar.

Scatter the watercress and tomatoes over a couple of plates and drizzle over a little olive oil and balsamic and season with a little salt and pepper.

Once the grill tray is really hot, remove the fish from the fridge, drizzle a little oil over the skin side and sprinkle generously with the salt. Take to the fire, along with the bowl of walnut crumbs.

Rest, skin-side down, onto the hot grill tray. Sprinkle the walnut crumbs over the top of the fish, patting down a little. The nuts will help prevent the fillets curling up but a gentle press down with a fish slice as they are cooking will also be helpful. Cook for just 3–5 minutes until the skin is super-crispy.

To serve, rest the fillets onto the salad and drizzle a little more oil and balsamic over the top.

Serves 4

4 x bass fillets, about 150g (5oz) each
a little olive oil, to drizzle
1 tbsp flaked sea salt

For the walnut crumbs

100g (3½oz/1 cup) walnuts
a good handful of parsley, about 20g (¾oz), roughly chopped
2 garlic cloves
flaked sea salt and freshly ground black pepper

To serve

a good handful of watercress per person
400g (14oz) really ripe vine tomatoes, sliced
4 tbsp good extra virgin olive oil
4 tbsp good balsamic vinegar

Red mullet with mouclade sauce

Red mullet have a slightly shellfish taste and they are one of my personal favourite fish. As usual, do take some time to dry out the fish skin for maximum crispiness. The sauce here is a riff on mouclade, a French dish of lightly curried mussels in a creamy sauce.

A good few hours before you want to cook, lay the fish fillets skin-side up on a rack hung over a tray and slide into the fridge uncovered to dry out the skin.

When you are ready to cook, light the barbecue ready for hot direct grilling and set a grill tray over the fire to heat up.

Wash the mussels under cold running water, discarding any that don't shut when you tap them gently against the sink. Pull off and discard any beards and put the mussels into a bowl.

Tip the mussels onto the grill tray and shut the lid, cooking for about 5 minutes until they have all opened. Discard any that refuse to open and scoop the rest onto a large plate or tray, allowing to cool for a couple of minutes before picking from their shells. Leave the grill tray over the fire ready to cook the fish.

Set a flameproof frying pan over the fire – it's fine on top of the grill tray – and add the butter. Tip in the leeks and sweat down for a good 10–15 minutes until they are soft but not really coloured. Add the garlic, curry paste and some salt and pepper to the leeks and cook for another couple of minutes. Pour in the wine and let it bubble away and reduce a little, then add the cream and most of the parsley. Bring the sauce to the boil, then stir through the mussels and slide off the heat to keep warm.

Drizzle a little oil over the skin side of the fish and sprinkle with the salt flakes. Rest skin-side down onto the hot grill tray and set another tray or pan on top to weigh the fillets down and stop them curling up (page 75). Grill for just a few minutes until the skin is crispy and the flesh is cooked. Remove the tray from the grill and use a fish slice to tease the fillets free.

To serve, spoon the sauce into warmed bowls and rest the fish, skin-side up, on top. Sprinkle over a little extra parsley.

Serves 2

4 mullet fillets, about 150g
   (5oz) each
a little olive oil
1 heaped tbsp flaked sea salt

For the mouclade sauce

500g (1lb 2oz) mussels
50g (2oz) butter
1 leek, finely chopped
2 garlic cloves, chopped
1–2 tsp good curry paste
125ml (4fl oz/½ cup) white wine
100ml (3½fl oz/scant ½ cup)
   double (heavy) cream
a loose handful of parsley, about
   10g (⅓oz), roughly chopped
flaked sea salt and freshly ground
   black pepper

Hake steaks with sherry and porcini sauce and roast Jerusalem artichokes

Hake steaks are different from fillets because they are cut into rings across the fish, each with a little disc of bone in the centre. They are also sometimes called cutlets.

Mushrooms with fish may seem a little wild, perhaps too earthy, but if you're sceptical, trust me. It works. The flavours here are slightly autumnal, dare I say hearty, making this a good dish to pick when the weather is a touch chillier. I would eat this with a simple green salad – maybe spinach and watercress – dressed with good extra virgin olive oil and a squeeze of lemon juice.

A couple of hours before you want to cook, rest the hake on a tray over a rack and slide uncovered into the fridge to dry a little. At the same time, put the porcini in a heatproof jug and pour over 250ml (8fl oz/1 cup) boiling water. Set aside to soak.

Fire up the barbecue ready for two-zone grilling, piling the charcoal over one half of the barbecue so you can control the heat under the artichokes, moving them between a direct and indirect fire (page 31). Place a grill tray over the fire so it gets hot while the artichokes are cooking.

While the fire is heating, scrub the artichokes really well under running water to remove any dirt lurking in the crevices. Cut into 1cm (½in) thick discs and tip into a roasting pan so they fit in a single layer. Scatter over the sage and drizzle on a couple of tablespoons of the olive oil, then season well with salt and pepper, tossing to coat.

Take the pan to the barbecue and rest onto the grill bars away from the fire and shut the lid. Cook for a good 20 minutes so they start to soften a little. Then slide the pan over the fire and cook for 10 minutes or so, with the lid down, to give them a little colour – it's absolutely fine to put the roasting pan on top of the grill tray you're heating ready for the fish. Keep moving the artichokes on and off the heat, stirring a few times to mix, until they are soft all the way through and crispy at the edges; they may take 50 minutes or even a little more in total.

Serves 4

4 x 200g (7oz) hake steaks (cutlets)
700g (1lb 9oz) Jerusalem artichokes
a few sprigs of sage, leaves picked and roughly chopped
4 tbsp olive oil
2 tbsp plain (all-purpose) flour

For the porcini and sherry sauce

25g (¾oz) dried porcini
1 tbsp olive oil
2 garlic cloves, sliced
75ml (2½fl oz/scant ⅓ cup) dry rich sherry, such as oloroso
100g (3½oz) butter, chopped into 1cm (½in) cubes
flaked sea salt and freshly ground black pepper

To serve

watercress and/or spinach
lemon juice

Slide the pan away from the heat where they should sit happily away from the fire, keeping warm while you make the sauce and cook the fish.

Use a slotted spoon to lift the porcini from the soaking water onto a board and chop roughly. Line a sieve with a couple of sheets of paper towel and hang over a bowl. Pour the soaking liquid through the sieve so that any grit is removed – a slightly irritating but necessary step to avoid nasty crunchy bits in your sauce. Take to the barbecue along with the rest of the sauce ingredients.

Set a flameproof pan directly over the fire – again it's fine to rest the pan on top of the heating grill tray – and pour in the olive oil. Add the garlic slices and fry for just a minute or so. Add the chopped porcini, the strained soaking liquor and the sherry and allow to bubble away and reduce for a few minutes. Leave the lid up at this stage and witness the power of oxygen to gets those coals going (see page 28) and get the sauce bubbling rapidly. Once the liquid has reduced by about half, add the butter a few cubes at a time, whisking it in as it melts. Season to taste with salt and pepper and slide away from the fire to keep warm – I would just rest the pan on top of the artichokes.

Sprinkle the flour on a plate and season well with salt and pepper. Toss the hake steaks in the flour so they are coated all over. Drizzle both sides with the remaining couple of tablespoons of olive oil and take to the barbecue.

Set the hake onto the hot grill tray over the fire. Cook over a high heat for 2–3 minutes until lightly coloured, then use a fish slice to ease them off the grill surface and flip over to cook the other side. Use a temperature probe to check for doneness – it should read 60°C (140°F) deep in the centre.

To serve, scatter the watercress between the plates, dressing with a little olive oil, and spoon over the artichokes. Top with the hake and spoon the sauce over the top, then give everything a little squeeze of lemon juice.

Red gurnard, creamy grilled tomato and kale linguine

Gurnard is a brilliant but rather underused fish. I'd go as far as to say it's one of my favourites, slightly sweet-tasting with firm flesh that holds together well. Whether you get the whole gurnard and fillet it yourself or ask your fishmonger to fillet it for you, definitely make stock from the bones (page 33). Gurnard makes very excellent stock. Good ripe tomatoes are a must here, giving you such a perfect balance of sweetness and tartness. If I have a big glut of tomatoes from my tiny greenhouse, I will roast up a whole load and freeze them in portion-sized bags. They are the most magic thing to find on a dark winter's night when you're rummaging around the freezer looking for something to cook. Similarly if you spot reduced 'yellow sticker' toms in mid summer, grab them, roast and freeze.

A few hours before you want to cook, spread the gurnard fillets out skin-side up on a rack hung over a tray to dry the skin out for 2–6 hours.

When you are ready to cook, fire up the barbecue with the charcoal piled on one half. Shut the air vents quite low to give you a steady temperature of around 140–150°C (284–302°F); see page 29 for lid temperatures.

Set a deep frying pan on the grill bars away from the fire and pour in a little olive oil. Add the onion and a good pinch of salt, stirring to coat the onion. Spread out the tomatoes in a small roasting pan and drizzle with a little more olive oil. Season well with salt and pepper and set onto the grill bars next to the onions. Shut the lid of the barbecue and leave both to cook gently for around 30 minutes, stirring the onions and rotating the tomato pan once or twice to make sure they are cooking evenly. You want to soften and intensify the flavours of both without adding too much colour.

While the onion and tomatoes are cooking, bring a large pan of salted water to the boil on the hob. Add the linguine and cook until just tender. Toss in the torn kale for the last 2–3 minutes of cooking, then drain well. Return to the pan and drizzle through just a little olive oil to stop the strands sticking together.

Serves 2, easily doubled

2 large red gurnard fillets, from a whole gurnard of about 750g (1lb 10oz)
olive oil, to drizzle
1 large onion, finely chopped
300g (10½oz) cherry vine tomatoes, halved
150–200g (5–7oz) dried linguine
125g (4oz) curly kale, leaves pulled from stalks and torn into bite-sized pieces
2 garlic cloves, sliced
a handful of tarragon, leaves picked and roughly chopped, plus extra to garnish
½–1 tsp dried chilli (hot pepper) flakes, or to taste
200ml (7fl oz/scant 1 cup) crème fraîche
flaked sea salt and freshly ground black pepper

Once the tomatoes are cooked, scoop them into the pan
of onions along with the garlic, tarragon and chilli. Slide the
pan towards the heat a little and stir briefly to fry the garlic.
Spoon in the crème fraîche, stirring to mix, then add the
cooked linguine and kale and toss well together. Slide off
the heat again to keep warm.

Set a grill tray on the grill bars above the fire and leave for
a few minutes to get hot.

Remove the fish from the fridge, drizzle a little oil all over and
sprinkle generously with flaked salt. Lightly brush oil over the
underside of a fish weight or heavy pan for weighing the fillets
down (page 75). Take to the barbecue and rest skin-side down
onto the hot grill tray, placing the oiled weight on top. Cook
directly over the heat, leaving the lid of the barbecue off so the
heat just comes from underneath (page 29) until the skin is
really crisp and you can see that the flesh of the fillet is starting
to flake. Remove the grill tray or cage and use a fish slice to tease
the fillets off. Slice each fillet in half.

To serve, pile the pasta between two warmed bowls and top
each with a couple of pieces of gurnard and scatter with the
remaining fresh tarragon.

Grilled mackerel, oregano and lemon pesto with Greek-style butter beans

Much as I love my fish and meat proteins, I adore pulses and try to eat them several times a week. Cheap and cheerful, a bowlful of beans is an excellent way of making your fish go a little further. Fresh oregano is one of my favourite herbs, giving a slightly floral note to this pesto-style dressing.

As is usual, a few hours before you want to cook, lay the mackerel fillets skin-side up on a rack over a tray and slide into the fridge to dry the skin and minimize sticking.

For the pesto, pour a good 4 tablespoons of the olive oil into a bowl and stir through the chopped oregano and garlic, the lemon zest and juice. Season to taste with salt and pepper and a good pinch of sugar. Spoon out a tablespoon or so into a separate small bowl ready to baste the fish, then set both bowls aside.

When you are ready to cook, fire up the barbecue ready for direct grilling but leaving an area coal-free so you have room to manoeuvre if things are getting hot. Set a grill tray or cage over the fire to heat up.

Once the fire has a little heat in it, start on the beans. Set a flameproof pan over the fire (it's fine to rest the pan on the grill tray so you can heat two things at once!) and pour in the olive oil. Add the tomatoes and garlic and fry for a few minutes, just until the tomatoes are softening. Add the beans and cinnamon, then season to taste with the sugar and salt and pepper. Bring up to a simmer and cook for a few minutes. Take the pan off the heat and cover with a lid or foil to keep warm – they are more flavourful eaten warm rather than hot, so don't worry too much about them cooling a little.

Remove the mackerel from the fridge and drizzle the remaining tablespoon of oil all over the skin side, spreading it out into a thin, even layer. Sprinkle generously with salt flakes and take to the grill along with the smaller bowl of pesto and a silicone brush.

Serves 2–4, depending on what else you are eating

4 mackerel fillets
75ml (5 tbsp) olive oil
a good bunch of oregano, about 20g (¾oz), leaves picked and finely chopped
2 garlic cloves, finely chopped
zest and juice of 1 lemon
a pinch of sugar, to taste
flaked sea salt and freshly ground black pepper

For the beans

3 tbsp olive oil
500g (1lb 2oz) ripe vine tomatoes, roughly chopped
2 garlic cloves, crushed to a paste
2 x 400g (14oz) cans of butter (lima) beans, drained and rinsed
1 tsp ground cinnamon
1–2 tsp sugar, to taste
flaked sea salt and freshly ground black pepper

Lay the fillets, skin-side down, on the hot grill tray and rest
a lightly oiled weight (page 75) on top to press the fillets flat,
keeping the skin in maximum contact with the hot surface.
After a couple of minutes, the weight will have done its job so
remove it, then brush the oregano pesto over the flesh side of the
fish. Cook for another couple of minutes until the skin is crisp.

Use a fish slice to tease the fillets from the grill tray and rest on
top of the beans. Drizzle over the rest of the pesto and tuck in.

Oat-crumbed herring and rhubarb sauce

Like all the oily fish, herring are best eaten super-fresh as fish fats go off quickly (pages 16–17). In this recipe you are best off cooking them in a hot pan over the fire with a generous quantity of sizzling butter, both for the flavour and so you don't lose the oats to the flames.

The rhubarb, though, does benefit from a bit of charring on the grill bars to intensify its flavour. Go gently with the honey in the sauce, a bit of tongue-curling sourness is just the job to cut through the rich fish.

Fire up the barbecue ready for direct grilling, setting a large flameproof frying pan on the grill bars to heat up.

Tip the oats and rosemary into a small food processor and season with salt and pepper. Pulse until roughly ground, then transfer to a large plate and spread out in a thin layer. Pour the milk into a shallow dish and rest the butterflied herring on a plate.

Drizzle just a little oil over the rhubarb stems and rest on the grill bars over the fire, sliding the heating frying pan out of the way to make space, if necessary. Grill for a few minutes, turning regularly, until lightly caramelized and softening. Remove and roughly chop into 1–2cm (½–¾in) pieces. Transfer to a small flameproof pan and add the honey, ginger and lemon juice. Set over the fire to melt the honey and cook the rhubarb so it begins to collapse. Add a touch more honey if you think it needs it but try to keep it sharpish! Remove from the heat.

Scatter the watercress over a couple of plates and dress with the lemon juice and a good drizzle of olive oil.

Take the plate of oatmeal, the milk and the herrings and have handy by the barbecue. Drop the butter into the hot pan and let it melt and sizzle.

Working quickly, dip the herrings into the milk to coat all over. Drop onto the plate of oatmeal and turn over to coat lightly in the crumbs before dropping into the hot butter. Cook for just 1–2 minutes each side until crisp and golden.

Pile the herrings onto the salad and serve with the sauce.

Serves 2

50g (2oz/heaped ⅓ cup) oats
1 tbsp fresh rosemary needles
    (picked from a couple of
    good sprigs)
4 tbsp milk
4 herring, butterflied, about
    100–125g (3½–4½oz) each
50g (2oz) butter, for frying
flaked sea salt and freshly ground
    black pepper

For the rhubarb sauce

250g (9oz) thinnish rhubarb
    stems (about 4–5)
a drizzle of olive oil
1–2 tbsp honey, to taste
1 tsp ground ginger
juice of ½ lemon

To serve

2 good handful of watercress
juice of ½ lemon
extra virgin olive oil

Trout fillets with roast red pepper pesto and grilled broccoli

Naturally oily, trout fillets are brilliant for grilling as they are not as prone to sticking compared to less rich-fleshed fish. I use small trout fillets for this, allowing a couple per person, but you could use one big fillet, about 500g (1lb 2oz), to share if you like.

Lay the trout fillets skin-side up on a rack hung over a tray and slide into the fridge uncovered for a few hours to dry out the skin and help prevent sticking.

When you are ready to cook, fire up the barbecue ready for hot direct grilling and set a grill tray over the fire to heat up.

As it heats up, rest the pepper over the building fire to roast – only do this if you have good pure charcoal (see page 12 for all that important info). If your fuel has chemicals in it, do the smell test. You need to wait until it is properly hot before cooking, and hopefully try and get better fuel for next time! Either way, you want to roast the pepper for a good 20 minutes or so until lightly charred all over. It's better to roast slowly so it softens properly without getting completely black, so slide it further from the heat if you need to. At the same time, set a small pan either over the fire or on the hob and toast the almonds for a few minutes until they are a couple of shades darker and smelling nutty.

Remove the pepper and allow to cool for a few minutes before peeling and discarding the skin, seeds and membranes. Drop the flesh into a food processor along with the toasted almonds, garlic, basil, parsley and olive oil and blitz to a paste. Season well with salt and pepper. You can also make this in a pestle and mortar for a chunkier finish. Scoop a tablespoon into a small bowl to take to the barbecue and the rest into a serving bowl and set aside.

Drizzle a little olive oil over the broccoli and the skin side of the trout fillets, and season both generously with salt and pepper. Spread the broccoli out over the grill tray and cook over a high heat until lightly charred. Pile away from the heat so it keeps warm.

Serves 2
2 trout, filleted, about 300g
   (10½oz) each
olive oil, to drizzle
200g (7oz) purple sprouting
   or tenderstem broccoli

For the pesto
1 red (bell) pepper
25g (¾oz/3 tbsp) blanched
   almonds
1–2 garlic cloves, whole, unpeeled
a small bunch of basil, about
   15g (½oz)
a loose handful of flat-leaf
   parsley, about 5g (⅛oz)
2 tbsp extra virgin olive oil
flaked sea salt and freshly ground
   black pepper

Rest the trout, skin-side down, on the grill tray and lay an oiled
fish weight or pan on top to stop it curling up (page 75). Cook
for a few minutes then remove the weight and use a silicone
brush to coat the flesh side with the reserved pesto. Cook for
another couple of minutes until the skin is crispy and eases away
from the grill tray when teased gently with a fish slice. The flesh
should be cooked by the time the skin is crisp as the fillets are
pretty thin.

To serve, divide the broccoli between warmed plates and top
with the fillets. Add a generous dollop of pesto and tuck in.

Ling wrapped in fig leaves with roast figs, chilli and coriander seed

I appreciate that fig leaves are pretty niche here – my apologies – but if you happen to have a fig tree (and I do), then the leaves make a wonderfully fragrant wrapper, especially if they are picked in early summer when the leaves are young and bright green. If you don't have access to fig leaves, don't bypass this recipe entirely; the roast figs make a lovely, unusual companion to simple, grilled, skin-on fillets of fish.

Lay the fig leaves in a shallow dish and pour over enough boiling water to cover. Set aside for a couple of minutes, then drain well. This will help them become softer and more pliable.

Spread the leaves out in 4 piles of 3 so they overlap and form something as close to a rectangle as you can make. Rest a piece of fish in the centre of each set of leaves and drizzle over the oil, tossing the fish over once or twice to coat. Season well all over with salt and pepper. Roll up the leaves to enclose the fish as best you can; it won't matter if a little is exposed. Use small skewers to pin the leaves through to hold them together and drizzle a little extra oil over the outside. At this point you can rest them, seam-side down, on a plate and slide into the fridge until you are ready to cook. They will be fine for up to 6–8 hours.

When you are ready to cook, light a charcoal or wood fire ready for hot direct grilling.

Take a small flameproof pan and set on the grill bars over the fire. Drop in the butter and allow it to melt, then add the figs, crushed coriander seeds and chilli. Season with a little salt and pepper and stir over the heat for a few minutes until the figs are lightly caramelized. Squeeze in the lemon juice and allow it to bubble and reduce until sticky, then slide off the heat.

Rest the fish parcels, seam-side down, on the hot grill bars and cook for 2–3 minutes on each side until the leaves are lightly charred and the fish is cooked through – check with a temperature probe; it should read 60°C (140°F).

Serve the parcels with the figs alongside.

Serves 4

12 young fig leaves, about
    hand sized
700g (1lb 9oz) ling fillet,
    cut into 4
3 tbsp olive oil
flaked sea salt and freshly ground
    black pepper

For the roast figs

50g (2oz) butter
250g (9oz) soft dried figs,
    chopped into 1cm
    (½in) pieces
1 heaped tbsp coriander seeds,
    crushed
1–2 tsp chipotle dried chilli
    (hot pepper) flakes, to taste
juice of 1 lemon

You also need a few small
    metal skewers

Spiced ray wings and squash couscous with lemon and oregano dressing

A dish inspired by Sicily, where Africa meets Europe and the food is full of Moorish influence, so you get spices and couscous alongside lemons and fresh herbs, a heady combination.

You may be more familiar with skate wings over ray wings – they are close relatives – but ray is a more sustainable choice. Indeed, when you buy skate in a fish shop or a restaurant, what you are probably eating is indeed a ray as skate is classified as vulnerable to overfishing. When you have finished eating, gather up the frames of the wings and save for stock, storing in the freezer is just fine for another day's job. A cartilaginous fish, the bones are absolutely loaded with gelatine and tasty goodness and they make excellent stock (page 32).

The ray wings should be already skinned – a job invariably done by the fishermen on the boat, but you may benefit from trimming them. Use sharp scissors to snip off just a little from the tips of the thinnest edge as they will just burn over the fire. Rest on a rack over a tray and dry in the fridge for a few hours.

In a small bowl, mix together the flour, cinnamon, nutmeg and a good seasoning of salt and pepper. Set aside until you are ready to cook the fish.

To make the dressing, pour the extra virgin olive oil into a small mixing bowl and stir through the onion, preserved lemon, oregano and capers. Add the lemon zest and juice and the honey to taste, along with a little salt and pepper and whisk together until combined. Set aside. If you want to get ahead, it will keep very happily for a few hours in the fridge – just give it a quick whisk up before using.

When you are ready to cook, fire up the barbecue ready for two-zone grilling, so you can cook direct and indirect. Set a fish cage or grill tray over the fire and leave to preheat until really hot while you cook the squash.

Drizzle a little olive oil over the squash and season with salt and pepper. Rest the slices on the grill bars away from the fire and leave to cook indirectly until soft, perhaps 30 minutes or so, shutting the lid of the barbecue to trap in that all-important

Serves 4

1kg (2lb 4oz) ray wings
50g (2oz) plain (all-purpose) flour
1 tbsp ground cinnamon
½ tsp freshly grated nutmeg
olive oil, to drizzle
flaked sea salt and freshly ground black pepper

For the dressing

100ml (3½fl oz/scant ½ cup) extra virgin olive oil
1 small red onion, very finely chopped
1 small preserved lemon, peel finely chopped (about 1 tbsp chopped peel)
a small handful of oregano, about 15–20g (½–¾oz), leaves picked and roughly chopped
2 tbsp capers, roughly chopped
zest and juice of 1 lemon
1–2 tsp honey, to taste
flaked sea salt and freshly ground black pepper

convection heat (page 29). Once soft when pierced with the tip of a knife, slide the slices over the fire and cook for a few more minutes, allowing them to lightly caramelize. Remove from the fire and chop into bite-sized pieces.

Once the squash is cooked, pour the couscous into a flameproof pan – a saucepan or even a deep enamel tin is great. Stir through the cooked squash, raisins and a generous grind of salt and pepper. Pour in the hot stock or water and a drizzle of olive oil. Give it a quick mix, then cover tightly with foil and take to the barbecue. Rest on the grill bars away from the fire so the couscous rehydrates and keeps warm while you cook the fish.

Sprinkle the spiced flour over a large plate and toss the wings in it to coat all over. Take to the barbecue and give them a good drizzle of olive oil just before resting onto the hot grill tray or in the fish cage. Cook for a few minutes on each side until golden and crisp, and a temperature probe reads 55°C (131°F) in the deepest part. Remove to a tray and take inside to rest for a few minutes while you grill the kale.

Lightly drizzle the kale stems with olive oil and season with salt and pepper. Grill directly over the fire for just 1–2 minutes until crispy. Cut the leaves from the tough stalks, roughly chopping as you go, and discard the stalks. Remove the pan of couscous from the barbecue and discard the foil. Scatter over the chopped leaves and toss together with a fork to fluff up the grains, then pile onto a serving platter.

Use a fish slice to tease the wings from the tray or cage and rest them over the couscous. Give the dressing a quick final whisk, then drizzle over the lot before serving.

For the couscous

1kg (2lb 4oz) squash, cut into 1cm (½in) slices, skin removed
250g (9oz/1⅓ cups) couscous
a handful of raisins, about 50g (2oz/heaped ⅓ cup)
250ml (9fl oz/1 cup) boiling hot fish stock or boiling water (use 1 stock cube, or even better homemade stock; see pages 33–35)
250g (9oz) kale stems

Leek-wrapped cod with almond saffron sauce

White fish fillets have a low fat content and are notoriously sticky. The leeks here act as an edible wrapper, both flavouring the fish and stopping it sticking to the grill surface.

If there are any Romesco sauce fans out there (I count myself here, I absolutely love it), you should definitely try this sauce. It does, however, need to be made fresh and eaten warm straight after you make it. Think of it like a sort of garlicky, nutty mayonnaise, but the nuts soak up too much liquid and make it stodgy if you leave it hanging around for too long. I love it so much I can eat it off a wooden spoon from the pan.

Trim both ends of the leeks a little. There's no need to trim off all the green – you can use it just fine. Slice each in half down the length and peel off the top 4 layers or so, saving the inside layers for a different recipe (try using in the stock base on page 33). Rinse the outer layers clean of any mud and lurking debris. Bring a large pan of salted water to the boil and add the leek strips – they won't fit, but just push them under the water gently as they soften, just as you would with spaghetti. Blanch for just a couple of minutes until floppy, then drain and rinse under cold running water to stop them cooking any further. Drain well.

Lay the strips out on a baking sheet in 4 piles of strips, each strip slightly overlapping the next. Pat dry with paper towel, then lift each pile and turn over, patting dry the other side. Reserve a few of the thyme leaves, then sprinkle most of them over the leeks and season well with salt and pepper. Place a fish fillet at one end of a pile and roll up snugly. Secure the join with a little metal skewer or cocktail stick (toothpick), then repeat with the other fillets. At this point you can chill in the fridge until you are ready to cook, or they will store for 24 hours.

Fire up the barbecue ready for direct high heat cooking (page 31) and set a grill tray or fish cage over the fire to heat up.

While the barbecue is heating, start to get the sauce ready. Pour the fish stock into a small saucepan and add the saffron. Set over a medium heat on the hob and bring to the boil, then simmer for 5 minutes. Turn the heat right down to keep hot.

Serves 4

2 large leeks
a good handful of thyme stems, leaves stripped
700g (1lb 9oz) chunky cod fillet, cut into 4
4 trusses of cherry tomatoes on the vine, about 5–6 tomatoes on each
olive oil, to drizzle
flaked sea salt and freshly ground black pepper

For the almond saffron sauce
250ml (9fl oz/1 cup) fish stock
a large pinch of saffron
2 tbsp olive oil
100g (3½oz/⅔ cup) blanched almonds
60g (2oz/1 cup) fresh breadcrumbs
a loose handful of flat-leaf parsley, about 10g (⅓oz)
2 fat garlic cloves
3 tbsp extra virgin olive oil

Set a frying pan over a medium heat and add the 2 tablespoons of olive oil. Once it's hot, add the blanched almonds and breadcrumbs and stir over the heat for a few minutes until crisp and golden. Stir through the parsley for the last minute or so to soften it a little. Tip into a food processor, add the garlic and a generous grind of salt and pepper and blitz until ground. Set aside to finish after you've cooked the fish.

When the barbecue is hot, drizzle a little oil over the leek fish parcels and tomatoes. Set the fish onto the hot grill tray or into the fish cage and rest the tomatoes over the heat until soft and lightly charred. Grill the fish over a high heat for a few minutes on each side until you get a reading of around 55°C (131°F) on a temperature probe. Remove to a tray and take inside to keep warm, along with the griddled tomatoes.

To finish the sauce, pour the hot stock into the food processor and blitz to a smooth paste. With the motor running, drizzle the extra virgin olive oil down the spout so it emulsifies to a thick, creamy sauce.

To serve, spoon the sauce onto warmed plates, spreading it out, then top each with a leek fish parcel. Tuck a truss of tomatoes alongside and sprinkle with the reserved thyme leaves.

Chapter 3:
Fish on a stick

We know that cooking fish can be occasionally irritating as it is a delicate protein that is prone to sticking and falling apart. Skewers, or 'fish on a stick', are perhaps the stickiest of them all, with small, slightly fragile pieces lined up on skewers, just ripe for falling off when you try to turn them. Head back to page 26 on fish proteins and how that makes them prone to sticking and for my top tips for alleviating the problem.

Some fish are naturally more sturdy than others – so with white fish, monkfish or ling both have a denser texture than cod, for example, and so will hold on to skewers better. The naturally more oily fish, like trout or mackerel, are also less prone to sticking. Tuna, with its meaty texture, is another great one to skewer. With shellfish, scallops and prawns also hold their shape well.

When it comes to the cooking, as is the mantra throughout this book, hot and clean is essential, so get that fire hot and scrub those bars before you even think about setting any skewers directly onto grill bars. You can also line up the skewers inside a fish cage or onto a grill tray, which can be better than setting them directly onto the grill bars, but, as usual, that cage or tray needs to be super-hot before it sees any fish, so make sure you heat it up really well.

There are also some other things that will definitely help. Don't try to turn the skewers too early, test an edge by trying to ease it up with a fish slice. If it's stuck, wait another minute and try again. Often the fish will unstick itself once it has had a chance to form a crisp, golden crust.

Perhaps my favourite tip is to ditch the grill bars altogether and use a couple of fire bricks to literally hang the skewers so they 'float' above the fire. You can see this in action on page 125, and fire bricks are pretty easy and cheap to pick up in DIY stores. Some barbecues, like some of the Weber kettles, for example, have a central circular section of grill bars that you can remove so you can float the skewers over. Or, if you are only cooking for one or two, how about lighting a fire in a chimney starter and hanging the skewers across the top of it?

Another rather nifty little tip is to add a piece of vegetable at either end of your skewer that is fractionally bigger – just by a few millimetres – in size than the fish pieces, which will just hold the fish a tiny bit above the grill bars so it's not actually in contact. A fairly chunky disc of courgette (zucchini) would be a perfect choice, as you can witness on page 122.

I also love to line up whole small oily fish – sardines or fresh anchovies – onto skewers simply because the skewers make them easier to turn over in one manoeuvre rather than turning individually. You can see this in action on page 70.

When it comes to the skewers themselves, I always, without fail, use the metal ones. The bamboo ones inevitably burn, even if you soak them in water, and the metal ones are endlessly usable rather than disposable. Lining up your food, be it fish or meat or vegetables, onto two skewers is also an excellent way to make them more structurally sound. A double skewer means when you go to turn them, the whole thing turns around rather than the food spinning about irritatingly on the stick. You can buy special double skewers, or you can simply use two per kebab.

Coriander tuna with red pepper mayo

Inspired by a Portuguese holiday, where grilled fish is everywhere and, for the most part, treated very simply indeed and none the worse for it. I would eat this with a big salad, crusty bread, maybe a squeeze of lemon and definitely glasses of cold wine. My local supermarket sells ready-cubed tuna that is really good value, presumably as it's a product of the trimming of bigger steaks.

Set a small pan over a medium heat on the hob and tip in the coriander seeds. Toast for 1–2 minutes then roughly grind in a pestle and mortar and tip into a mixing bowl. Add the olive oil, season generously with salt and pepper and stir together. Add the chopped tuna and spring onions and toss to mix. Thread onto skewers and set aside on a plate. Slide into the fridge for an hour or two to marinate.

When you are ready to cook, fire up your barbecue ready for hot direct grilling.

While the coals are cooking to a good fish temperature (page 31), set the red pepper over the heat and leave to char and soften all over. At the same time, rest the bay leaves on the grill bars and let them lightly char for just a few seconds before removing. Transfer the pepper to a bowl, cover with a plate and leave for 10 minutes so the steam loosens the skin. Peel the blackened skin away, then cut in half, discarding the seeds, membranes and stalk. Drop the flesh into a mini food processor. Remove the central rib from the cooked bay leaves and roughly chop, then add to the processor along with the garlic and chilli, if using. Blitz until smooth, transfer to a bowl and leave to go cold. Once cold, fold through the mayonnaise. You can also really finely chop everything for a slightly coarser sauce, but don't add to the mayo until cold.

Once the fuel is ready to cook on, give the grill bars a really good scrub with a stiff wire brush before resting the skewers over the fire. You can also deploy one of the kebab cooking strategies on page 113. Grill the skewers for a few minutes until lightly crisp all over, then remove to a warm plate.

Scatter over the coriander and serve with the mayo alongside.

Makes 6 skewers

2 tbsp coriander seeds
3 tbsp olive oil
600g (1lb 5oz) tuna steak, chopped into 2–3cm (¾–1¼in) pieces
1 bunch of spring onions (scallions), cut into 2–3cm (¾–1¼in) lengths
flaked sea salt and freshly ground black pepper

For the red pepper mayo

1 red (bell) pepper
2 fresh bay leaves
2 garlic cloves, peeled
1 red chilli, seeds in or out (optional, to taste)
100g (3½oz/scant ½ cup) mayonnaise

To garnish

coriander (cilantro), chopped

You also need 6 metal skewers

Trout, asparagus and orange with mint garlic oil

Simple colourful little skewers using diced trout fillet, which my daughter rather reluctantly agreed were 'as nice as salmon'. Head on back to page 11 to read my case for trout as a way better choice than salmon. When asparagus is not in season, sub in tenderstem or purple sprouting broccoli. As is often the case, a little fresh herby hint post cooking, this time via a minty oil, really elevates the whole dish.

Dice the trout into 3cm (1¼in) chunks. If you have thinner sections on one side of the fillets you can stack them to make thicker pieces. Cut the asparagus into similar-sized lengths. Leaving the skin on, slice the orange in half, then into quarters and cut into little wedges.

Thread everything alternately onto metal skewers, double skewering if you can to make life easier for yourself (page 113). Drizzle generously with the olive oil and season all over with salt and pepper. At this point you can slide into the fridge for a few hours until you are ready to cook.

Fire up the barbecue ready for hot direct grilling, letting the coals fully burn, and set a grill tray over the fire to get hot.

Scoop the mint leaves into a small bowl. Stir through the olive oil, garlic and red wine vinegar and season with salt and pepper to taste. Set aside.

Take the skewers to the grill and set on the hot grill tray. Cook for a couple of minutes each side until the trout is golden and crisp. Try to avoid turning the skewers until the crust has formed to minimize the chance of sticking.

Serve drizzled with the mint oil, and don't forget to nibble the orange flesh off the skin as you eat.

Serves 4

500–600g (1lb 2oz–1lb 6oz) chunky trout fillets, skinned
200g (7oz) asparagus, washed and trimmed
1 orange
2 tbsp olive oil
flaked sea salt and freshly ground black pepper

For the mint garlic oil

a good handful of mint leaves, about 15g (½oz), finely chopped
100ml (3½fl oz/scant ½ cup) olive oil
1 garlic clove, crushed to a paste
1–2 tsp red wine vinegar, to taste

You also need 8 metal skewers

FISH AND PULSES

The following two recipes feature a generous non-fish element by way of pulses, both as a delicious and nutritious part of the dish but also as a thrifty way to make a little expensive fish go a bit further. Kinder on the wallet as well as a more sustainable way to enjoy fish following the 'buy better, eat less' rule I have learnt to always use in meat cookery.

I have made both these equally well with ling or monkfish and consider them fairly interchangeable options. Ling, however, is a little harder to source but it is more sustainable than monkfish, so ask your fishmonger to get it in for you. The more people see it around, the more likely they are to cook with it. Any chunky-cut white fish – cod, pollack or haddock – would be good for these recipes but be aware the texture makes them a little more delicate.

Monkfish sumac skewers with warm chickpea purée, spinach and burnt lemon

Sumac is a lovely lemony-tart spice popular in Middle Eastern cooking that works particularly well with fish dishes. You can also use it as a post-cooking seasoning in the same way you would salt and pepper. If you wanted to carb-up this dish, some warm flatbreads torn and dipped into the chickpeas would be an excellent addition.

Tip the diced fish into a bowl and pour the olive oil over the top. Sprinkle in the sumac and season well with salt and pepper. Toss until evenly coated, then thread onto the skewers. Line up on a plate or tray and slide into the fridge to marinate for 30 minutes to 2 hours.

When you are ready to cook, fire up the barbecue for hot direct grilling, but leaving a portion of your grill surface fire-free so you have heat control (page 31). You can cook the skewers on a hot grill tray or cage or hang them as described on page 113.

For the chickpeas, set a flameproof pan – a small, deep frying pan is ideal – directly over the fire. Pour in a couple of tablespoons of the olive oil and add the chickpeas, garlic and crushed cumin. Grate in the zest from both lemons, then slice the fruit in half and set the cut faces down on the grill over the fire. Leave to lightly burn on the cut face, then slide off the heat to keep warm. Stir the chickpeas and cook for 10 or so minutes until sizzling and lightly coloured in places. Scoop into a bowl.

Serves 4

600g (1lb 5oz) monkfish fillet, diced into 3–4cm (1¼–1½in) cubes
3 tbsp olive oil
3 tbsp sumac
flaked sea salt and freshly ground black pepper

Pour the remaining tablespoon of olive oil into the pan and slide onto the grill bars away from the fire. Add the washed spinach and a sprinkle of chilli flakes. Shut the lid of the barbecue so the spinach wilts a little – I like to cook it lightly so the leaves soften but retain their shape – it should happily wilt by itself.

Meanwhile, tip most of the chickpeas into a food processor, saving a couple of tablespoons to garnish. Spoon in the tahini paste and pour in the boiling water. Whizz to a smooth purée and set aside while you cook the fish.

Remove the fish skewers from the fridge and take to the barbecue. Raise the lid and give the spinach a little stir. Rest the skewers onto a hot grill tray or hang them and cook for a couple of minutes on each side until lightly charred. Remove, along with the burnt lemon and wilted spinach.

To serve, spoon the chickpea purée between two warmed plates and scatter over the reserved whole chickpeas. Divide the spinach between the plates and top with the skewers. Drizzle generously with extra virgin olive oil and squeeze over the burnt lemon. Sprinkle with coriander or parsley and serve warm.

For the chickpeas and spinach

3 tbsp olive oil
2 x 400g (14oz) cans of chickpeas (garbanzos), drained
3 garlic cloves, chopped
2 tbsp cumin seeds, roughly crushed
2 lemons
200g (7oz) fresh spinach leaves, washed and shaken dry
a good pinch of dried chilli (hot pepper) flakes
5 tbsp tahini paste
100ml (3½fl oz/scant ½ cup) boiling water

To serve

a drizzle of extra virgin olive oil
a little coriander (cilantro) or parsley, roughly chopped
toasted pittas or flatbreads (optional)

You also need 8 metal skewers

Tandoori fish skewers and red lentils with curry leaf butter

Here the yogurt in the marinade makes the sticking situation harder, so head back to page 113 to remind yourself of the best options for cooking fish kebabs. I make the lentils first ahead of time on the hob in the kitchen for utter convenience, often making a double batch to stash leftovers in the fridge because a bowl of lentils with a dollop of yogurt and a handful of fresh herbs is my go-to desk lunch for the working week. The curry leaf butter is best made fresh.

For the lentils, put the onion, garlic, ginger and turmeric in a food processor and blitz to a paste.

Set a large pan over a low heat on the hob and pour in a tablespoon of oil. Add the onion paste and cook gently to soften, about 10 minutes. Tip in the lentils and pour over enough cold water to come 2cm (¾in) above their level. Stir together and simmer for about 50–60 minutes until soft. You may well need to add a splash more water. Once cooked, season well with salt and pepper and set aside ready to reheat.

Tip the cumin and coriander seeds into a small pan and toast for a minute or two until they smell fragrant. Tip into a pestle and mortar and grind to a coarse powder, then pour into a mixing bowl. Add the yogurt, lemon juice, garlic, ginger, turmeric, paprika and chilli along with a good grind of salt and pepper. Stir well to mix, gently fold through the fish cubes, then thread onto your skewers. Slide into the fridge to marinate for an hour.

When you are ready to cook, fire up the barbecue ready for hot direct grilling (page 31).

Set a small flameproof pan over the fire and drop in the butter to melt. Add the fresh curry leaves and chillies and allow to sizzle and bubble for a few minutes to crisp up. While the butter is cooking, warm up the lentils – either on the hob or over the fire.

Drizzle the skewers generously with oil and grill for a few minutes each side.

To serve, spoon the warmed lentils generously onto warmed plates, top with a skewer and drizzle with the butter.

Serves 4

For the red lentils
1 onion, roughly chopped
3 garlic cloves
25g (¾oz) ginger, roughly chopped
25g (¾oz) fresh turmeric, roughly chopped, or 1 tsp ground
vegetable oil
300g (10½oz/1¼ cups) red lentils
flaked sea salt and freshly ground black pepper

For the skewers
2 tbsp cumin seeds
2 tbsp coriander seeds
75g (2½oz) full-fat natural yogurt
juice of 1 lemon
3 garlic cloves, crushed to a paste
25g (¾oz) ginger, grated
25g (¾oz) fresh turmeric, grated, or 1 tsp ground
2 tsp sweet paprika
1–2 tsp chilli powder, or to taste
600g (1lb 5oz) firm white fish, cut into 4cm (11/2in) cubes
vegetable oil, to drizzle

For the curry butter
100g (3½oz) butter
a few sprigs of curry leaves (you want a good handful)
2–3 red chillies, sliced, or to taste

You also need 8 metal skewers

FISH ON A STICK

Monkfish teriyaki skewers with pickled cucumber

Genuine teriyaki is always made with chicken, so consider this an inauthentic but delicious fishy version. These little skewers make a great nibble before your main course, but you could also serve them with rice as a more substantial offering. They are very quick and easy to cook so begin with the pickle and the tare (a basting and dipping sauce), then it's just a question of a quick grill and baste.

For the pickle, trim off the ends of the cucumber and slice down the middle lengthways. Take a teaspoon and run it down the cut side of each half to scoop out and discard the seeds. Lay the halves cut-side down and slice finely into 2–3mm (⅛in) half-moons, scooping into a bowl as you go. Stir through the rice wine vinegar, sugar and salt.

Set a small pan on the hob over a medium heat and tip in the sesame seeds. Toast for a few minutes until golden, keeping an eye on them as they can suddenly burn, then tip into the bowl with the cucumber. Stir together and set aside.

To make the tare, pour the sake, mirin and soy into a small pan set over a low heat. Add the ginger, garlic and plenty of black pepper. Stir for around 5 minutes until slightly reduced. Divide between two small bowls, one for the baste and one for the dipping sauce, and set aside to go completely cold.

When you are ready to cook, fire up the barbecue ready for direct grilling. These are so quick to cook you won't need much fuel here unless you are going on to cook something else.

Thread the chopped monkfish onto metal skewers – here I've deployed the courgette tactic (page 113) to raise the fish off the grill bars – and take to the fire along with the bowl of basting sauce and a silicone brush. Grill the kebabs for just a couple of minutes each side, basting as you go.

Serve hot from the grill with the dipping sauce and pickled cucumber alongside.

Makes 8 small skewers
600g (1lb 5oz) monkfish fillet,
    chopped into 2–3cm
    (¾–1¼in) cubes

For the pickled cucumber
1 cucumber
3 tbsp rice wine vinegar
2 tsp caster (superfine) sugar
2 tsp flaked sea salt
2 tbsp sesame seeds

For the tare
100ml (3½fl oz/scant ½ cup) sake
100ml (3½fl oz/scant ½ cup)
    mirin
100ml (3½fl oz/scant ½ cup)
    soy sauce
25g (¾oz) ginger root,
    finely grated
2 garlic cloves, crushed to a paste
freshly ground black pepper,
    to taste

You also need 8 metal skewers

Turmeric ling skewers with lime leaves and chilli-peanut brittle

I think of these as a great little bar snack, just the sort of salty, sweet, spicy nibble I want with a cold glass of something nice before I cook the rest of the meal. You could also serve them as a main course with rice.

Ling can be a little more of a 'sticker' than monkfish so do get your grill hot and squeaky clean, and I would consider grilling suspended over the fire if you can (see opposite). You could, of course, substitute monkfish if you prefer but, currently at the time of writing, ling is a cheaper and more sustainable option (see page 10 for more on general fish sustainability).

Begin with the brittle as it needs time to set and cool. You could make it 24 hours in advance and store it in an airtight tin. Spread a sheet of baking parchment over a baking tray and set aside.

Weigh the sugar into a small heavy-based saucepan and add the salt and a couple of tablespoons of cold water. Set on the hob over a medium–low heat and allow to melt and caramelize to a dark amber colour. Swirl the pan gently round as it melts – it should take 10 minutes or so but do stay with it because it can turn quite quickly once it starts – resist the temptation to stir, though, as this can cause the sugar to recrystallize. If you have a thermometer (page 23) it's a really useful thing for caramel – you are looking for the 'hard crack' stage, which is 149°C (300°F). Once it has caramelized, reduce the heat to a minimum and tip in the peanuts, chilli and soy sauce and stir together. The soy will cause the caramel to seize into hard lumps, but don't stress, just stir over a really low heat until it remelts. Once it is all smooth again, pour on the prepared baking tray and quickly level out into a shallow layer. Set aside to go completely cold and hard.

Put the fish cubes into a bowl and add half the oil, turmeric, garlic and a generous seasoning of salt and pepper. Toss gently together to coat, then slide into the fridge for 30 minutes to marinate.

Fire the up the barbecue ready for hot direct grilling (page 31).

Makes 8 skewers to serve 4–6 as snack, fewer as a main meal

For the chilli-peanut brittle
75g (2½oz) caster (superfine) sugar
½ tsp flaked sea salt
50g (2oz/⅓ cup) peanuts
2–3 bird's-eye chillies, finely chopped, to taste
1 tbsp soy sauce

For the fish
700g (1lb 9oz) ling fillet, chopped into 3cm (1¼in) cubes
4 tbsp vegetable oil
25g (¾oz) fresh turmeric root, grated
2 garlic cloves, crushed to a paste
5 double-lobed fresh lime leaves (10 leaves)
flaked sea salt and freshly ground black pepper

To serve
2 limes, quartered

You also need 8 metal skewers

While the grill is heating, take the cold brittle and chop up quite finely into little pieces, around 3–5mm (¼in). Scoop into a bowl ready for serving.

Tear each lime leaf in half, discarding the tough central stem, then tear each half in half again to give you little pieces. Thread the fish onto skewers, adding little pieces of lime leaf between the pieces. Drizzle the rest of the oil over the skewers, brushing it well all over so they are evenly coated.

Grill over a high heat for just a couple of minutes until lightly charred in places. To serve, pile onto a warm plate and sprinkle over the peanut brittle pieces. Tuck in the lime wedges to squeeze over as you eat.

Fish kofta with burnt aubergine salad

For this recipe the cut or species of fish is unimportant. Any fish and any bits and bobs will do and if you have been filleting and prepping your own fish (pages 18–21), perhaps you have some scrapings and 'fish mince' squirrelled away in the freezer. Or maybe, just maybe, your fishmonger will have some bargain trimmings they are prepared to sell you. A word of warning: do give yourself time for the freezing step, as they will be practically impossible to cook while soft.

The aubergine salad here is another example of fish 'upselling' by adding a tasty accompaniment to bulk out the fish and make your pennies go further.

Tip the onion and garlic into a food processor and pulse to finely chop. Add the fish, eggs, breadcrumbs, lemon zest, oregano and allspice. Season well with salt and pepper and pulse to a gluey paste. Scoop onto a large plate and divide into 8 even-sized balls. Wash your hands!

Lay a sheet of baking parchment onto a tray and have the skewers handy. Lightly wet your hands with cold water, then scoop up a ball and pat it into a long oval torpedo shape, aiming for banana thickness. Insert a skewer down through the centre and lay it on the baking sheet. Repeat. The mixture will be very sticky and feel, perhaps, impossibly sloppy but stay with it; wet hands will help, so if you are getting in a muddle, stop and rewash them. Once you have shaped all the kofta, slide the tray into the freezer to chill for at least 2 hours. You cook them from frozen so it doesn't matter if you leave them longer – they will store, well wrapped, for a couple of months.

When you are ready to cook, fire up the barbecue ready for direct grilling, setting a grill tray over the fire to heat up. You can cook the veg for the salad while the fire is getting fish-hot – but only if your charcoal is top notch, which I hope it is (page 12). I often add a little wood to get a subtle smoke hit into them as they grill.

Makes 8 kofta, to serve 4–6

1 small onion, roughly chopped
2 garlic cloves, roughly chopped
700g (1lb 9oz) fish trimmings –
    mixed white and/or oily fish
2 eggs
50g (2oz/1 cup) fresh breadcrumbs
zest of 1 lemon (save the juice
    for the salad)
a few sprigs of oregano, about
    15g (½oz), leaves picked
1 tsp ground allspice
olive oil, to drizzle
flaked sea salt and freshly ground
    black pepper

Drizzle a little oil over the aubergine slices and tomato halves and season with a little salt and pepper. Rest on the grill tray and cook until lightly charred and soft all the way through – the aubergines may take a little longer than the tomatoes. Remove from the grill tray and leave to cool slightly before chopping into 1cm (½in) pieces and tipping into a mixing bowl. Stir through the garlic, oregano, lemon juice and extra virgin olive oil and season to taste with salt and pepper.

Wash the grill tray and set it back over the fire to heat up ready for the koftes.

Remove the skewers from the freezer and drizzle a little oil all over, using a brush or clean hands to make sure they are fully coated. Rest on the hot grill tray over the fire and cook for 2–3 minutes on each side until they are golden and cooked through – a temperature probe will reassure you that the centre is hot; it should read 60°C (140°F).

Spoon the salad into a serving bowl and top with a generous dollop of Greek yogurt. Lay the kofta onto a plate. Add a final drizzle of extra virgin olive oil and a sprinkle of oregano to both just before serving.

For the burnt aubergine salad

3 large aubergines (eggplants), cut into 2cm (1in) slices
250g (9oz) ripe vine tomatoes, halved
1–2 garlic cloves, crushed to a paste
a few sprigs of oregano, about 125g (½oz), leaves picked and chopped
juice of 1 lemon (from above)
2–3 tbsp extra virgin olive oil, to taste

To serve

200g (7oz/scant 1 cup) Greek yogurt
extra virgin olive oil
a few extra oregano leaves, roughly chopped

You also need 8 metal skewers; double-pronged ones are handy if you have them (page 113)

Fresh anchovy escabeche

Trust me, and I mean this in a good way, these grilled then marinated anchovies are like the best canned fish you've ever had and they are excellent smushed into hot toasted sourdough and drizzled with plenty of extra virgin olive oil. They are cooked whole; I think life's too short to master filleting an anchovy. To eat, just grab the head and pull gently, bringing the backbone along with it to discard. The vinegary dressing softens the fine bones over time so much that there's little need to worry too much about them when you are eating and, besides, they contain bags of good nutrients.

Fresh anchovies are not the easiest to source, arriving sporadically but prolifically when they do. Most are destined to be salted and cured, but eaten fresh they are a real treat. Sardines would make a great alternative. Either way, they will happily keep in the fridge for 3 days or so.

To make the escabeche sauce, pour the olive oil into a saucepan and set over a low heat. Add the onion, carrot, garlic, fennel and chilli flakes. Cook gently for a good 20 minutes until the veg are really soft but not particularly coloured. Squeeze in the tomato purée and stir for a minute or so before pouring in the wine, vinegar, sugar and water. Bring to the boil and simmer for 5 minutes before removing from the heat and setting aside while you cook the fish.

If your fishmonger hasn't done so already, you need to gut the anchovies, which is very simple and can be done without the need for a knife. Hold a fish in the palm of your non-dominant hand and slide the tip of your thumb on the other hand in behind the gills, pulling the mouth forward and down and the guts should follow easily. You can twist off the whole head at the same time but I prefer to just take the lower jaw and guts and save removing the head and backbone until after they have marinated. Repeat with the remaining fish and wipe inside and out with paper towel. Avoid washing, as wet skin will always stick more than dry skin, and will not go crispy.

Serves 4–6 as a starter or snack

2 tbsp olive oil
1 red onion, finely chopped
1 carrot, finely chopped
2 garlic cloves, finely sliced
1 heaped tsp fennel seeds, bruised in a pestle and mortar
½ tsp dried chilli (hot pepper) flakes
1 tbsp tomato purée (paste)
3 tbsp white wine
3 tbsp white wine vinegar
1 tbsp sugar
100ml (3½fl oz/scant ½ cup) water
500g (1lb 2oz) fresh anchovies
2 tbsp flaked sea salt
freshly ground black pepper

To serve
extra virgin olive oil

You also need 6 metal skewers

Once all the fish are gutted, line them up in two rows with all the heads facing one way. Take one skewer and pierce through the centre of one of the rows of fish so they are all connected together. Take the second skewer and thread it through the head end, and the third skewer through the tail end, so you have a neat silvery slab of anchovies. Repeat with the other row of fish and other three skewers.

Fire up your barbecue so it's hot and ready for direct grilling, allowing the embers to burn fully (page 31).

Sprinkle the fish liberally with the salt and grill over a high heat for just a couple of minutes on each side until charred all over. They will collapse and fall off the skewers if you overcook so get that fire nice and hot and work fast. Anchovies are small and delicate so I would definitely consider deploying one of the anti-sticking skewer techniques described on page 26.

Once cooked, ease the fish off the skewers into a shallow dish where they will fit into a snug single layer. Season with a little pepper. Pour over the escabeche, spreading it evenly over the fish. Cover and refrigerate for at least 24 hours before eating cold, drizzled with plenty of extra virgin olive oil.

Butterflied sardines, stuffed with raisin and caper crumbs

One of my favourite little fish to grill, a touch fiddly to assemble but very speedy to cook and make a great lunch or snack. The crumbly crispy filling will very much want to fall out so cooking these on a perforated grill tray is a great idea because you will minimize bits lost to the fire. You could also cook them on a chapa or in a frying pan but you would lose a little of that smoky charm from a direct hit of heat from the fire.

You will also need about 8 metal skewers. The double-skewer trick is especially good here to keep everything secure (page 113).

Set a small frying pan over a medium high heat on the hob, or indeed onto the barbecue above the fire if you already have one lit. Pour in the olive oil and add the breadcrumbs and thyme leaves, frying for a few minutes until golden and crispy. Stir through the garlic, raisins and capers and season with a little chilli flakes, if using, along with a grind of salt and pepper. Fry for another minute or so just to cook the garlic a little, then tip into a bowl to cool.

Get the barbecue ready for direct grilling and set a grill tray over the fire to heat up.

Spread out the sardine fillets skin-side down on a board, lining them up snugly together, and sprinkle over the crumbs. Starting at the head end of each fillet, roll up tightly towards the tail. When they are all rolled, thread a double row of skewers through to secure them shut – you should be able to line up 3 or 4 rolls per skewer depending on the size.

Drizzle with olive oil and sprinkle over a little salt, then rest on the hot grill tray. Cook for a couple of minutes on each side until crispy. Serve immediately.

Serves 2–4, depending on what else you are eating

2 tbsp olive oil
50g (2oz/1 cup) fresh breadcrumbs
a few sprigs of thyme, leaves picked
1 garlic clove, chopped
40g (1½oz/⅓ cup) raisins, chopped
2 tbsp capers, chopped
1–2 tbsp dried chilli (hot pepper) flakes (optional)
16 sardines, butterfly filleted (page 20), or buy them ready butterflied from the fishmonger
a drizzle of olive oil
flaked sea salt and freshly ground black pepper

You also need 8–10 metal skewers

Scallop, chorizo and sage skewers

These ridiculously easy and very tasty skewers take just a couple of minutes to cook, so plan on making them as part of a bigger spread to get the most out of your good fuel. They make a lovely little nibble while you're cooking your main course. It can be a little tricky to source, but you could also make these using morcilla, a delicious Spanish black pudding, if you can find some.

Fire up the barbecue ready for hot direct grilling but, as usual, leaving a fire-free zone on your grill so you can slide the skewers further from the heat.

Use a small sharp knife to separate the orangey-pink coral from the scallop and drop both into a bowl. Add the chorizo, sage, garlic and olive oil. Season generously with salt and pepper and stir well to coat.

Starting and ending with chorizo (the more solid texture of which will hold everything else in place), alternately thread the skewers up with the scallop, roe and sausage. At this point you can chill in the fridge for 30–60 minutes, if you like.

When you are ready to cook, rest the skewers directly over the fire, either hung between two bricks as I did here, or onto hot clean grill bars. Grill for just a minute or so on each side until lightly caramelized. The fat from the chorizo will cause the fire to flare a little so if it's all getting a bit much, slide a little further away from the fire.

Squeeze over some lemon juice and tuck in while sizzling hot.

Makes 6 skewers

12 fat scallops
200g (7oz) fresh cooking chorizo,
     cut into bite-sized pieces
a loose handful of sage leaves,
     finely chopped
2 garlic cloves, finely chopped
2 tbsp olive oil
flaked sea salt and freshly ground
     black pepper

To serve

1 lemon, cut into wedges

You also need 6 metal skewers

Prosciutto, prawn and mangetout skewers with lemon chive mayo

Surf, turf and crunch, these are such a tasty treat. Wrapping the prawns is easy but a little time consuming, you'll soon find rhythm, and the good news is you can make up the skewers well ahead of time where they will happily sit in the fridge for a few hours. The mayo can be mixed up at the same time and chilled, then the cooking is all over in a matter of a few short minutes.

I refer you on to page 240 for a word on prawn sourcing.

Tip the drained prawns onto a couple of sheets of paper towel and pat dry.

Take a slice of prosciutto and cut it into quarters to give you 4 small rectangles. Then wrap a prawn in one of the pieces so it's snugly contained in a prosciutto blanket. Repeat until all the prawns are wrapped.

Thread a prawn onto one of the skewers, followed by a mangetout, piercing it through the flat side, followed by another prawn. Keep on threading until you have used everything up, then brush a little oil all over each skewer and season with salt and pepper. Refrigerate until you are ready to cook.

Spoon the mayonnaise into a small bowl and stir through the lemon zest and chives. Add lemon juice to taste, starting with half the lemon and adding a little more if you like. Season with a little salt and plenty of pepper. Chill until needed.

When you are ready to cook, fire up your barbecue ready for hot direct grilling. Once hot, give the grill bars a really good scrub clean with a wire brush.

Rest the skewers on the grill bars over the fire and cook for 1–2 minutes on each side until the ham is golden and the prawns are pink. Serve immediately with the mayo alongside.

Makes 4–6 skewers

300g (10½oz) raw peeled king prawns (jumbo shrimp), drained
10 slices of prosciutto
150g (5oz) mangetout (snow peas)
1 tbsp olive oil
flaked sea salt and freshly ground black pepper

For the lemon chive mayo

125g (4oz/½ cup) mayonnaise
zest of 1 lemon, and juice to taste
10g (⅓oz) chives

You also need 8–12 metal skewers – I like to use double skewers here (page 113)

Chapter 4: Smoked: hot and cold

Smoke and fish are such natural partners and there is a beautifully long history of humans across the globe flavouring and preserving their food by curing and smoking it.

This history perhaps creates some mystique around smoking, but all it involves is adding wood smoke to food, and you can do this with very minimal extra kit on top of your lidded barbecue. Remember that good charcoal (and I refer you back to page 12 – perhaps the most important paragraph of this whole book) does not, should not, smoke and it will not make your food taste smoky. So if you want smoke, you need wood.

There are two types of smoking, hot and cold.

Hot smoking is where you add smoke flavour and cook food simultaneously, so the finished product is ready to eat. Hot smoking is usually the far quicker of the two options because you bypass a long cure in salt.

Cold smoking is all about getting maximum smoke into the food while leaving it in its uncooked state, either ready to eat raw, or ready to cook, so you use a gentle trickle of smoke over a long period of time but without generating any heat. Cold smoking should always be done in conditions of under 30°C (86°F).

Each section that follows will give you the detail you need on kit and technique.

Also with these smoked fish recipes, consider not discarding the skin once you've sliced up the fillet, as it is packed full of flavour and good nutrients. Rest it skin-side down in a hot pan on the hob with a fish weight or smaller pan on top and fry until crisp. It's great munched on its own, like a fishy crisp, or crumbled up and used as a smoky sprinkle on top of salads – particularly excellent on a potato salad.

HOT SMOKING

There are just a slim three recipes in this chapter that are hot smoked, plus the Smoked fish hotdogs (page 193) and the Smoked mussels with panko and thyme crumbs (page 219). But really, you could add a little smoke flavour to any of the recipes in the book. If that smoky taste is your thing, go for it, experiment away. The big whole fish – turbot and brill in particular – would take beautifully to a bit of smoke wood, and the recipes in the Fish in a Pan chapter (starting on page 244) would all be grand cooked over an open wood fire for a smoky hint.

How to hot smoke

You need no special kit over and above your usual barbecue kit, as all you are doing is adding wood smoke on top of the charcoal you are using for heat. You can cook on a pure wood open fire and your food will taste smoky, but if you want the full-on smoked experience, something with a lid is really advantageous to trap in the smoke.

Think cool not hot!

Fish is cooked when it gets to a 60°C (140°F) internal temperature and, once proteins are cooked, smoke is no longer able to be absorbed. Therefore the more time you take getting your fish to a cooked state, the more smoky it will taste. Fish proteins cook much quicker than meat proteins (page 26) so you need to keep things gentle. This is why hot smoking is always best done in pretty cool conditions – try to keep your barbecue running at around 120°C (248°F), otherwise the fish cooks before the smoke has done much of its magic – yet another reason that a lidded barbecue is your friend over an open fire. With an open fire, you have no control over the oxygen flow, so your fire will burn hot and your food will cook quickly. A lid with vents allows you to slow, slow, slow the burn down, moderating the temperature so the food takes longer to be cooked, resulting in a much more smoky flavour.

What type of wood for hot smoking?

I always buy small, fist-sized chunks over little wood chips. The chips burn super-fast because they have a big surface area to volume ratio, so you either need to keep adding them (expensive, irritating) or you can slow down the burn by soaking in water (resulting in dirty wet smoke, not great for taste nor planet). The aim of the game here is to get maximum smoke in a relatively short time, and a couple of fist-sized chunks of wood popped on top of a small lit fire will smoulder away nicely.

With regard to what species of wood to choose, I urge you not to stress too much, as the smoke taste is just a layer of flavour in the finished dish. I generally grab oak or one of the fruit woods like apple or cherry. Pick a wood and experiment with the quantity of smoke you like. Personal tolerance of smoke is similar to that of salt or chilli; some people gravitate to more, while some definitely like less. Find out where you and your family are on that scale, then once you've mastered that, maybe try a different wood species to see how that grabs you. Smoking food should be fun not prescriptive, and I certainly won't advocate only using certain species of wood for certain types of food.

HOT SMOKED FISH PÂTÉS

The following two recipes are entirely interchangeable in that you can make the rillettes with mackerel and the smooth pâté with trout and they will be equally delicious. Both employ the same hot smoking technique, that is light a little charcoal and add a little wood for smoke. For gentle cooking and maximum smoke absorption, a barbecue temperature of around 120°C (248°F) is ideal.

Post smoking, if you have time, rest the fish pâté in the fridge overnight. This will give you a more smoky taste as smoke molecules will still travel from surface to the centre over a period of hours. Don't worry if you're in a rush though – it will still taste great.

In both cases, it's useful to rest the fish on a grill tray or fish cage to smoke (page 24) to help you lift the delicate cooked fish off the grill at the end of cooking. If you have neither, a sheet of foil or even baking parchment pierced all over with a sharp knife to let some smoke through, is a good alternative. Because you are cooking over a low, indirect heat with the fish far from the fire you don't need to worry that the paper will catch fire.

Devilled hot smoked trout rillettes

A supremely easy, chunky, smoky, buttery thing, brilliant scooped onto hot toast or crispy crackers. The layer of melted butter sets on the surface and seals the fish from the air; providing it's submerged and sealed, it will keep for at least a couple of weeks. Once you crack the seal and let the air in, eat within 3 days. If you feel you won't eat it that quickly, consider packing it into a series of individual ramekins.

This recipe uses pul biber, or Aleppo pepper, which adds a vibrant red colour and a little heat. I like things spicy so add a little hot chilli pepper too. Pul biber is a very abundant spice in Turkish and Syrian cooking and becoming much more readily available. If you can't get it, substitute with paprika and a little chilli for punch.

Rest the filleted fish in a single snug layer in a baking dish, skin-side down.

Set a small frying pan over a medium heat on the hob and tip in the pul biber, fennel, peppercorns and chilli flakes (if using). Toast for a minute or so to wake them up, then tip into a pestle and mortar and crush roughly. Stir through the salt, then sprinkle all over the flesh side of the trout, pressing down a little with your palm so they get maximum contact. Slide the tray uncovered into the fridge and leave for an hour or so. You can make it up to 6 hours ahead.

Serves 4–6

1kg (2lb 4oz) whole trout (either one large or several smaller ones), filleted, or about 600–650g (1lb 5oz–1lb 7oz) trout fillets
2 tbsp pul biber
1 heaped tbsp fennel seeds
1 tsp black peppercorns, toasted and ground

When you are ready to cook, fire up your barbecue for hot smoking, shutting your air vents down to aim for a gentle indirect heat of around 120°C (248°F). Slide the fish skin-side down onto a grill tray or fish cage, or a piece of foil or baking parchment pierced all over to allow the smoke access to the underside.

When your barbecue is up to temperature, rest the fish skin-side down onto the grill bars as far from the fire as you can so it cooks gently. Shut the lid and leave to cook for around 30–40 minutes, or until the fish flakes easily when teased with a fork. If you have a probe, the internal temperature should be 60°C (140°F). Remove and set aside to cool to room temperature.

Use your fingers to break the fish into flakes, keeping an eye out for sneaky little pin bones that you may have missed. If you find any, pull them out and discard along with the skin (or follow the tip on page 138 for crispy nibbles!). Pack the flakes into a large serving bowl, individual ramekins or a couple of Kilner (Mason) jars if you have them. Pour over the melted butter so it completely covers the fish. Slide into the fridge to completely chill and set the butter.

1 tsp dried chilli (hot pepper) flakes (optional)
2 tsp flaked sea salt
150–200g (5–7oz) butter, melted (enough to cover the fish completely)

Hot smoked mackerel pâté

Mackerel pâté reminds me of being young, as Mum used to make it often with ready-smoked peppered mackerel fillets – which indeed you could also do for a more instant kind of gratification. But taking super-fresh, beautiful mackerel, filleting, salting and smoking it yourself is a very satisfying thing to do.

Sprinkle the salt all over the mackerel fillets and rest on a rack, skin-side up, hung over a tray. Slide into the fridge for an hour or two to lightly cure.

Set up your barbecue ready for gentle smoking, adding 2–3 lumps of smoking wood, and shut the vents right down to limit the airflow so you have a temperature of around 120°C (248°F).

Rest the mackerel skin side down on the grill bars away from the fire – use a hot fish cage or grilling basket if you have one – and smoke for around 30–40 minutes, or until the fish flakes easily with a fork. If you have a probe, the internal temperature of the fish should read 60°C (140°F). Remove and set aside to cool to room temperature.

Flake the fish from the skin and drop into a blender, taking care to spot and remove any little pin bones that may have been missed during filleting.

Add the butter, crème fraîche, horseradish, mustard and lemon juice, along with a generous grind of black pepper. Whizz to a smooth purée, then taste, adding a little more horseradish, lemon juice, salt and pepper as necessary.

Stir through the chives, spoon into a serving dish and chill until required. This pâté will keep for 3 days or so in the fridge.

Serves 4–6

1 tbsp flaked sea salt
1kg (2lb 4oz) mackerel, filleted (or about 600g (1lb 5oz) filleted mackerel)
150g (5oz) unsalted butter, chopped
2 tbsp crème fraîche
1–2 tbsp horseradish sauce, or to taste
1 tbsp Dijon mustard
½–1 lemon, to taste
a small bunch of chives, snipped
freshly ground black pepper

Smoked confit tuna salad with anchovy mayo

Slow smoking tuna in a bath of olive oil results in succulent smoky fish. As is often the way with smoking, an overnight rest in the fridge post-smoke is a good idea to allow the flavours to permeate and mellow, so do start this recipe the day before if you have time. I like to make the mayo in a pestle and mortar. With a single egg yolk, the volume is not large enough for a blender, and besides, there is something rather lovely about the slow, gentle process, knowing that you can actually do it like this.

Fire up the barbecue ready for gentle indirect smoking, aiming for a temperature of around 120°C (248°F) and add a few lumps of smoking wood of your choice (page 139).

Take a heatproof pan or dish that fits the tuna snugly. Pour in the oil and add the strips of lemon peel, the bay leaves, peppercorns and a good seasoning of salt, stirring to mix. Add the tuna, pressing in under the oil. It should be just covered in a layer of oil, depending on the shape of the fillet and the size of your dish, so add a splash more if you need to.

Set the dish on the grill bars as far from the fire as you can, shut the lid and leave to smoke gently for 1 hour. As long as the tuna is underneath the oil bath there should be no need to lift the lid and check – just let the smoke do its thing. Then remove from the barbecue and allow to cool completely in the oil. At this stage you can refrigerate, still in the oil, for up to 3 days.

When you are ready to eat, lift the tuna from the oil and set aside on a plate. Pour the oil into a jug (measuring cup); you should have about 100ml (3½fl oz/scant ½ cup). A little more or a little less is just fine.

Put the garlic and anchovies in a pestle and mortar and pound to a paste. Add the egg yolk and mustard and mix really well using a round-and-round motion with the pestle. Begin to drip in the smoked oil, literally a drop at a time to begin with, all the time mixing with the same round-and-round motion against the base of the mortar. Once you've incorporated a couple of tablespoons of oil you will be able to add it in a thin stream, but take your time. If you add it too fast you risk splitting the emulsion; it will be a good 10 minutes of stirring so enjoy the process. Once all the oil has been absorbed, season to taste with plenty of pepper and chill until needed. You can also use a mixing bowl and a balloon whisk, using the same slowly-slowly method.

Serves 2

For the tuna
125–150ml (4–5fl oz/½–scant ⅔ cup) olive oil, enough to cover the fish completely
a few wide strips of zest peeled from 1 lemon; save the juice to squeeze over the salad
2–3 bay leaves
200g (7oz) tuna steak, about 1cm (½in) thick
1 tsp black peppercorns
a sprinkle of flaked sea salt

For the mayo
1 fat garlic clove, roughly chopped
3 anchovy fillets in oil, drained
1 egg yolk
1 tbsp Dijon mustard
100ml (3½fl oz/scant ½ cup) smoked olive oil, drained from the smoked tuna
freshly ground black pepper

Add the potatoes to a pan of cold water and bring to the boil. Cook until tender, then drain. Add the beans to a pan and cover with boiling water, cook until just tender, then drain. Boil the eggs to your liking, with a hard or slightly jammy yolk, then run under cold water to cool a little before peeling and slicing in half.

Take two shallow bowls and put the lettuce leaves in the bottom, then squeeze over a little juice from the reserved lemon. Add the drained potatoes and green beans and tuck in the egg halves. Break the tuna into large chunks and add to the salad. Scatter over the olives and parsley and spoon over a dollop of mayo, serving the rest in a bowl alongside.

For the salad

250g (9oz) new potatoes, halved
200g (7oz) green beans, topped
    and tailed
2 eggs
2 little gem lettuce, leaves
    separated
a good handful of black olives
a loose handful of flat-leaf
    parsley, chopped

COLD SMOKING

First, a warning. Once you get the cold smoking bug it may be difficult to buy smoked fish again. It's such a pleasing activity, the smell of cold smoke is beautiful, and the end result tastes insane. The good news is it's very easy indeed; you will need a little time on your hands for curing and for the smoke to waft around your food and get absorbed, but once your smoker is running it's very hands-off.

Cold smoking is seen as more of a colder-weather activity. You wouldn't want food to be sitting out of the fridge under high ambient temperatures for the 12 hours or so it might take to smoke a whole side of trout, for example. In the warmer months you can keep the inside of your smoker relatively cool by tucking an old tray or bowl filled with ice somewhere inside the smoker and you can also smoke overnight when the air temperatures are cooler.

The power of salt

Salt, or sodium chloride, is a powerful little wonder molecule that boosts flavours and is a natural tenderizer. There is not a single recipe in this book that doesn't use salt to a greater or lesser extent, but in smoking, especially cold smoking, salt is critical to the curing process that makes smoked foods last longer and gives you that texture we associate with something like smoked salmon.

Over time, and at a high enough concentration, salt will reduce the water content in food, and if there's less water fewer bacteria are able to survive, so when you are curing fish – the trout recipe on page 148 is a classic example – you need enough salt over, on and around the fish to be absorbed into the fish cells, thus forcing the water out. However, in all honesty, curing and smoking in the modern refrigerator age is more about texture, flavour and cultural influences than lengthy food preservation.

There can be huge discrepancies in salt content from recipe to recipe. As a rule of thumb, if you are going to eat it raw you need more of a curing level of salt, while if you are going to cook it post smoking, you just need salt for seasoning.

What sort of salt you use is up to you. Sodium chloride is pretty much sodium chloride and different salts will not add differences by way of flavours, so it becomes about the texture and about personal choice. I always favour Maldon flaked sea salt for general sprinkling, but for the proper curing recipes that use a large quantity I would use fine table salt.

As a general rule I far prefer a dry brine (so just salt on its own) to a wet brine (when the salt is dissolved in water) as you use less salt and it's less faff. Wet brines work quicker, which is why they are often more commercially deployed.

The 'pellicle'

A rather lovely little word, this describes the sticky surface that comes from salting, or curing, followed by a drying period. The pellicle is a layer of dissolved myosin, a type of protein that forms on the surface. It will help the smoke molecules stick to the fish, so the forming of a pellicle is an important part of the process, making the drying step particularly important.

Cold smoking kit

I have a sweet little cupboard smoker made for me by my friend Gordon. Wire racks replace the shelves, there are hooks to hang fillets and a couple of little air vents to allow the all-important oxygen to circulate. I set a small cold-smoke generator on the base. Mine is like a little maze, made by Pro-Q, which I fill with smoking wood sawdust and light via a standard tea light. The smoke drifts around as the dust burns slowly round the maze – it can be alight for 12 hours or more and is a good bit of kit to get if you fancy trying cold smoking regularly.

That is not to say you can't cold smoke in a more ad-hoc way. At its most reductionist, you just need something that generates the smoke. You can improvise by filling an old metal pastry cutter with dust and lighting the centre, or by making a foil parcel filled with dust and pricked to create air holes. Both these ways will work fine, but you will need to refill with dust during the process, as the smoulder rate is less controllable. A maze means you can smoke unattended overnight when it is cooler. Then you need something that will contain the smoke – so something with a lid. I have seen people use a box, a metal bin or bucket, or an old filing cabinet – a swift search on the internet will reveal all sorts of ingenious cold-smoke set-ups. You can also use an empty barbecue or Kamado oven very successfully, but you need to make sure there is no old charcoal that might catch light, causing a hot rather than cold smoke. Whatever you choose will need just a little bit of venting so that air can get in and out, otherwise the fire will go out.

What wood for cold smoking?

In cold smoking you always choose a wood sawdust over bigger chunks or even chips of wood, as it simply produces more smoke at lower temperatures. Remember you are looking for smoke but not heat. It gets pressed down in a smoke generator or in your ad-hoc smoke system (see above) to minimize air gaps. So in effect you are reducing oxygen to hamper the combustion process and produce a slow, smouldering smoky little fire to flavour your food. This is why cold smoking takes time.

Cold smoked foods are often more of a pure product and eaten simply, unadorned with dressings and herbs and the like. Therefore, taste variations between different wood species are a touch more pronounced, so it's worth experimenting with different woods to see what you like. Personally I still favour the oak, apple or cherry trio I use for hot smoking – just in dust rather than chunk form – although maple and birch both give a nice light scented smoke.

The case for smoking other things

If you haven't got a smoker full of fish and you have some extra space, do think about chucking in something else alongside to maximize your smoke. I often just throw in a block of Cheddar alongside the fish where it will smoke very happily for as long as the fish is in. Excellent used to top the fish pie on page 165. Feta and Camembert are also excellent smoked, as is a whole unpeeled bulb of garlic, a block of butter or a shallow dish of extra virgin olive oil. You just need to have a little think about health and safety, as the food you smoke is often eaten in its raw state so keeping everything uncontaminated is a necessary step. Just lay things out so they can't touch or drip onto each other.

Classic cured and smoked trout

Trout in the smoked salmon style is a very delicious thing, just as good, if not better, than smoked salmon and definitely a better choice on a sustainability scale. It's also supremely satisfying and much more economical to make yourself than buying ready-cured and sliced fish. If you have salmon, the method and recipe is exactly the same, but I gently urge you to give trout a try. You'll find my trout-case set out on page 11.

The curing process is about ratios of cure weight to fish weight – following a basic rule of a 50% cure to fish, and a cure comprising of four parts salt to one part sugar. So if your fish fillet was 1kg (2lb 4oz), or 1,000 grams, you would be looking for a cure weight of 500g (1lb 2oz), made up of 400g (14oz) fine salt and 100g (3½oz) sugar. Or for a slightly more complicated set of figures (definitely using my calculator now – maths is a weakness!): if my fish is 750g (1lb 10oz), I need a total cure weight of 375g (13oz). I then divide the cure weight by 5, giving me 75g (2½oz), and I therefore need 4 × 75g (2½oz) salt and 1 × 75g (2½oz) sugar.

Bear in mind that smaller fillets of fish will cure quicker and be more prone to drying out, so I would recommend buying big if you can. Often, if you are buying trout online direct from the farms – see page 266 for a list of my favourite suppliers – you can specify the size, either of the whole fish that you fillet yourself, or a ready-filleted side. A larger piece of fish will obviously give you larger, more generous slices when you come to eat it, which is a bonus.

Take the trout fillet, rest it on a board and trim off any very thin, flappy bits from along the belly edge – these will over-cure and become very dry. Weigh the trimmed fillet, then use that weight to calculate your cure weight, as explained above.

Weigh the salt and sugar into a bowl and mix really well; clean dry hands are the best tool for the job. Take a dish that will fit the fish in a flat snug layer and sprinkle over about a quarter of the cure, then rest the fish skin-side down on top. Sprinkle the rest of the cure over the fish, making it a little thick at the fatter end and a little less at the tail end. Slide into the fridge and leave to cure for 6–24 hours. If you cure for less time you will end up with a softer slice of smoked fish to eat; a longer cure will give you a firmer slice – it's a question of personal preference. I prefer it on the softer side so would rarely cure beyond 12 hours.

Once cured, take to the sink, wash the fillet under cold running water, then pat dry with paper towels. At this point you can use fish tweezers to pull out any little pin bones; it's an easier job to do after curing. Rest skin-side down on a rack hung over a tray and slide into the fridge, uncovered, for a further 12 hours to develop the pellicle.

1 large side of trout, skin on
fine salt
dark soft brown sugar

When you are ready to smoke, hang or rest the fish horizontally in your chosen smoker (see page 147) and light your cold smoke generator. Leave to smoke for about 10–12 hours.

Remove the fish and wrap snugly in baking parchment. Slide into the fridge and leave for another 12–24 hours before eating – this will allow time for the smoke molecules to penetrate all the way through the fish and mellow out the flavours.

To serve, rest the fish on a board and use a sharp filleting knife to carve thin slices on the diagonal. The first slice will be a little too dry to eat fresh, as may any of the thinner edges and around the tail end where the flesh is quite thin. Don't waste these trimmings, though; just pile them into a freezer bag or container and freeze ready to use sparingly, like a seasoning, during cooking – they will be particularly excellent added to the Smoked fish pie (page 166) and would add a smoky nip to Classic fishcakes (page 169).

Once smoked, I would store my cured fish in the fridge and eat, like any fresh food, within 3–5 days. You can also slice the fillet and freeze slices in meal-sized portions, well wrapped in greaseproof (waxed) paper, then bagged or boxed. It will keep happily for up to 3 months.

SMOKED: HOT AND COLD

Beetroot and caraway smoked cured trout

A smoky riff on Swedish gravadlax, which traditionally is unsmoked and buried in the ground to cure. Caraway is such an interesting and somewhat underused spice, I love it here with the crazy-hued beetroot. I prefer to use raw beetroot for this, but ready-cooked beetroot would work fine too – you would just get a slightly more subdued colour.

If your trout, or trout fillets, are a slightly different weight to this it won't matter too much. If they are wildly different, adjust the cure quantities accordingly. This recipe follows the same method of curing as in the classic cured trout recipe on the previous page, so refer back for size and cure calculations.

Again, the proportions are the important thing, so I haven't given you a specific serving quantity.

Choose a dish that will fit the fish fillet in a snug flat layer.

Roughly chop the beetroot and drop into a mini food processor along with a couple of tablespoons of cold water; there's no need to peel. Omit the water if you are using ready-cooked beets. Whizz to a pulp, then add the salt, sugar and toasted and ground caraway. Blitz to mix, then spoon about a quarter into the dish, spreading it out into a thin layer. Rest the trout fillet on top, skin-side down, pushing it down flat. Spoon the rest of the cure mix onto the fish, spreading it out and pressing it down so that the cure gets maximum contact with the fish. Slide into the fridge to cure for 12–24 hours. The longer you leave it, the pinker the result, but it will also get firmer to the touch.

Take out of the fridge and rinse off the cure. Pat dry with paper towels and use fish tweezers to remove any pin bones. Rest on a rack hung over a tray. Slide back into the fridge and leave to dry for another 12 hours, to allow time for the pellicle to develop.

Smoke, rest and slice in exactly the same way as for the Classic cured and smoked trout (page 148).

250g (9oz) raw beetroot (or cooked, but definitely not packed in vinegar!)
300g (10½oz) fine salt
75g (2½oz/⅓ cup) caster (superfine) sugar
2 tbsp caraway seeds, toasted and roughly ground
about 750g (1lb 10oz) trout side, filleted

Cold smoked cod roe and real taramasalata

If you are not familiar with taramasalata I would describe it as a smoky, fishy mayonnaise, perfect for dunking bread or veg in, or spreading onto crackers. I love it. So many of my favourite foods take me back to high days and holidays. That's just one of the best things about cooking and eating for me: the memories attached to certain foods. Proper tarama – by which I mean not vivid pink and out of a supermarket tub – reminds me of lazy barefoot beachside lunches in Greece where you order way too much food for one sitting. And probably a few icy cold beers too, knowing me.

You can buy smoked roes and cut out the cold smoking stage but if you fancy a go, ask your fishmonger to get you in some fresh cod roe. Begin this recipe a couple of days before you want to eat it as the roes take time to cure, smoke and rest. A note on the olive oil: choose an oil you love the taste of in its raw unadulterated state. I like the tastebud wham of a strong extra virgin oil, but you may prefer something milder.

Take a dish that fits the roes in a single snug layer and sprinkle in half the salt. Lay the roe on top and sprinkle over the rest of the salt. Cure in the fridge for 12 hours.

Rinse the salt off under cold running water, then pat dry with paper towels. Rest on a rack hung over a tray and slide into the fridge, uncovered, to allow a sticky pellicle to form on the surface; 6–24 hours is fine, depending on the time you have. When you are ready to smoke, light your cold smoke generator in your chosen smoker (page 147) and smoke the roes on a rack for 12 hours. Remove from the smoker and refrigerate for another 12–24 hours to allow the smoke to 'set' and soak all the way through the roe.

For the taramasalata, put the whole piece of bread in a bowl and cover with cold water. Set aside to soak for 15–20 minutes, then lift the bread out and squeeze out most of the water. Drop into a food processor with the onion and garlic.

Use a sharp knife to slice open the smoked roes and scoop out into the food processor. Discard the skin. Squeeze in the juice of half a lemon and season really well with black pepper. Blitz well until smooth.

Makes enough for about 6–8 as a snack

For smoking the roe
100g (3½oz) fine salt
2 whole fresh cod roe, about 400g (14oz)

For the taramasalata
150g (5oz) piece of stale white bread, crusts removed
½ small red onion, roughly chopped
1–2 garlic cloves, to taste
about 300g (10½oz) smoked cod roe, from above
½–1 lemon, juiced, to taste
125ml (4fl oz/½ cup) extra virgin olive oil
freshly ground black pepper

To serve
Flatbreads and black olives

Then, with the motor running, pour in the olive oil in a slow, thin stream until it is all combined and emulsified into a creamy paste. Taste to see if you need to add any more lemon juice. You won't need any salt because of the curing process.

Scoop into a bowl and refrigerate for a few hours to allow the flavours to mellow out. It will store, covered, in the fridge for a good 3–4 days. I like to drizzle mine with more olive oil and a good grind of black pepper before serving alongside flatbreads and black olives.

TWO COLD SMOKED FISH
IN THE 'CEVICHE' STYLE

The following two recipes take the principles of a ceviche, whereby fish is lightly cooked in citrus acids, and add an irresistible, smoky edge. The astute may notice that in both recipes there is no rinsing off the cure and leaving the pellicle to form. I have used lower levels of salt, and the cure and pellicle stage happen together. The result is a softer texture and a more gentle smoky hit than the long-cured smoked trout, for example. After smoking, I would still urge you to try and rest the fish in the fridge for 12 hours before eating to allow the smoke molecules to soak all the way to the centre of the fillets.

Using the freshest of fresh fish is important here, especially with the mackerel because its high unsaturated fat content means it deteriorates quickly (page 16).

With both recipes you can eat the fish as a pre-dinner nibble, spooned onto crisp crackers or into little lettuce leaves. Or you can plate up as a starter or main course with some salad leaves, or just grab a fork and tuck in on its own.

Mackerel tartare with pickled ginger, cucumber, citrus and sesame

Contrasts are what rock this dish – smoky cold fish, soft and tender on the bite, astringent pickled ginger bringing heat and oomph, sweetness from the citrus, crunch from the cucumber and – maybe the best bit – hot toasty sesame seeds.

Rest the filleted mackerel on a rack hung over a tray, flesh-side up, and sprinkle over the salt evenly, crumbling the salt in your fingers to crush it a little as you go. Slide the uncovered tray into the fridge and leave for 6–12 hours to cure.

When you are ready to smoke, light your smoker. If you can hang the fish vertically in your smoker, pierce through the tail end of each fish with a hook and hang them. Otherwise, rest directly on the racking, skin-side down. Shut the door and leave to smoke for a good few hours. There are no rules here; quite simply more time will result in a smokier, firmer-textured fish. I think 4 hours would be a minimum and maybe 8–10 hours a maximum.

Remove the fish from the smoker and wrap tightly in greaseproof (waxed) paper, then slide into the fridge for another 12 hours or so to allow time for the smoke to even out through the fish.

Once the fish is out of the smoker, make the pickled ginger, as it benefits from a good rest in the fridge before eating. Use a teaspoon to scrape the skin off the ginger – a remarkably effective tool for the job – then take a vegetable peeler and peel the ginger into slivers, dropping them into a small bowl as you go. Heat the vinegar in a small pan and stir through the sugar and salt until dissolved. Pour the hot vinegar over the ginger slivers and stir to mix, pressing the ginger under the liquid as best you can. Cover the bowl and put it into the fridge alongside the fish.

Serves 4 as a starter, more as a nibble, fewer as a main course salad
4 large mackerel fillets
2 tsp flaked sea salt
2 satsumas or clementines
½ cucumber
3 tbsp sesame seeds
a few chives, finely chopped
freshly ground black pepper

For the pickled ginger
50g (2oz) ginger root
4 tbsp rice vinegar
2 tbsp caster (superfine) sugar
½ tsp flaked sea salt

The next day, unwrap the fish and rest it on a board. Use a super-sharp knife to carve it on the diagonal into 5mm (¼in) thin slices down to the skin. Dice up the slices into 1–2cm (½–¾in) pieces and drop them into a mixing bowl. Discard the skin or pan-fry it in a hot pan for crunchy sprinkles (page 138).

Use a microplane or the small holes of a box grater to finely grate the citrus zest into the bowl. Peel the fruit and remove as much pith as you can, then cut each segment into 5mm (¼in) pieces, dropping them into the bowl as you go. Dice the cucumber into 5mm (¼in) cubes and add. Pour over the ginger and pickling liquid and season well with black pepper. Stir really well to mix, then slide into the fridge for 30 minutes.

Just before you are ready to serve, set a small pan over a medium heat on the hob and toast the sesame seeds until deep golden brown. Whichever way you are serving the tartare (see page 154), tip over the hot sesame seeds just before eating to get that all-important contrast between hot and cold. Finally scatter over the chives and tuck in.

Maple cured bass with lime and tequila dressing

A little sweet, a little smoky, with a citrus and tequila hit, this is such a good way to enjoy really fresh wild bass when they come into season.

In a small bowl, mix together the maple syrup, salt and smoked paprika. Lay the fish in a shallow bowl or tray and pour over the cure, brushing it all over both sides of the fillets. Slide into the fridge and leave to cure uncovered for 6–12 hours.

When you are ready to smoke, follow the instructions on page 155 for the cold smoked mackerel tartare, smoking for 4–12 hours depending on the level of smoke you like. Wrap and rest in the fridge for 12 hours to let the smoke even out through the fish.

After the rest, unwrap and lay the bass skin-side down on a board. Use a really sharp knife to cut into thin slices on the diagonal and spread out on a platter in a single layer.

Mix the lime juice and tequila with the sugar and red onion in a small bowl, then pour over the fish slices. Slide into the fridge and leave to cure for 30 minutes.

Sprinkle with the chilli and herbs and drizzle generously with extra virgin olive oil. Finish with a good grind of black pepper before serving.

Serves 4 as a starter, more as a nibble, less as a main course salad

60ml (2fl oz/¼ cup) dark maple syrup
2 tsp flaked sea salt
1 tsp hot smoked paprika
600g (1lb 5oz) bass fillets, preferably wild caught in season
juice of 3 limes
2 tbsp tequila
2 tsp caster sugar, or to taste
½ red onion, very finely sliced
1–2 fresh red chillies, finely chopped
a few sprigs of coriander (cilantro), chopped
a few sprigs of mint, chopped
a good drizzle of extra virgin olive oil
freshly ground black pepper

Home smoked kippers with dulse soda farls and poached eggs

Herrings are medium-sized silver, oily fish, bigger than a sardine but smaller than a mackerel, and when smoked, they are known as kippers. They are traditionally cured in a wet brine – no doubt for commercial reasons as it's a quicker process – so that is what I have done here.

They make the perfect treat for brunch with poached eggs, along with speedy farls – a pan-cooked soda bread that's some sort of easy genius thing I wish I learned about sooner. For extra flavour (not to mention bonus nutrients!), I've added dried dulse, a type of seaweed, along with some wild garlic. You could leave out one or both, or substitute other herbs, like chopped chives or parsley.

Start this a couple of days or so before you want to eat, as the curing, drying, smoking and resting takes a little time but not a great deal of effort. For Sunday brunch, I would follow a timeline something like this: Friday late afternoon, quickly cure and dry the herring for a few hours, ready for an overnight 12-hour smoke, say 11pm to 11am or so; pull out, wrap and refrigerate until Sunday morning.

Measure the salt into a large baking dish or tray, something big enough to fit the herrings in a single flat layer. Pour in the water and stir well until the salt is completely dissolved. Lay the herrings in the brine, skin-side up and leave for 15 minutes.

Lift from the brine, rinse briefly under cold water, then pat dry with paper towels. Rest on a rack hung over a tray skin-side down, and slide into the fridge to dry out the surface for a few hours – 4 or 5 would be perfect, as they are quite small fish.

Set up your cold smoker (page 147) and hang or rest the herrings inside. Shut the door and leave to cold smoke for 12 hours. Remove from the smoker, wrap tightly in baking parchment and slide into the fridge to rest for a good few hours – overnight is ideal – this will help the smoke work its way all the way through the flesh so is a step worth doing.

The next day, when you are ready to cook, decide if you are cooking inside or outside. This is the perfect thing to cook in the garden on a nice morning, either over an open fire or on the grill bars of a barbecue, but you can just as well cook it on the hob in the kitchen too. If you opt for fire, you need a good heat but also, as always, room to manoeuvre food away if it's cooking too quick or too hot.

Serves 4

200g (7oz) fine salt
1 litre (34fl oz/4 cups) water
4 good-sized herrings, about
    100g (3½oz) each, butterflied
50g (2oz) butter, for frying

For the soda farls

250g (9oz/2 cups) plain
    (all-purpose) flour
1 tsp bicarbonate of soda
    (baking soda)
2 dried dulse, snipped into little
    pieces with scissors
15g (½oz) wild garlic – a handful
    – or chives, snipped
200ml (7fl oz/scant 1 cup) milk
juice of ½ lemon
flaked sea salt and freshly ground
    black pepper

For the farls, weigh the flour into a mixing bowl and stir through the bicarbonate of soda, dulse and wild garlic (if using). Season well with salt and pepper. Set a heavy-based skillet over a medium-low heat to get hot. Then pour the milk into a jug and stir through the lemon juice before pouring over the flour. Stir together briefly, no need to over mix. Tip onto a generously floured board and pat into a round of about 20cm (8in). Sprinkle more flour over the top – the dough will be quite wet and sticky, so do your best not to handle it too much. Gently does it.

Once the pan is hot, carefully slide the farl into it – no need for any oil or butter. Use a blunt knife or pizza dough cutter to cut through into quarters. Cook for about 7–8 minutes, then use a fish slice to flip over in the pan and cook on the other side, again for 7–8 minutes. Slide the pan off the heat and leave to rest while you cook the kippers and poach the eggs.

For the poached eggs, set a deep frying pan of cold water over the heat (fire or hob) and let it come up to a very gentle simmer. Crack an egg into a small glass and very gently slide it into the pan at low level so it just slithers in. No dropping, no swirling the water, just let it move under its own gravity. Repeat with the other eggs and let them sit in the barely simmering water until they are done to your liking, then remove with a slotted spoon to allow the water to drain away. Timings are tricky here but reckon on something like 2–5 minutes – the age of the egg matters, how cold it is matters. I advise just a little prod with a finger to gauge how soft the centre is. Softer equals runnier, firmer is harder – simple.

At the same time you set the egg water to boil, set a large frying pan over the heat and drop in the butter. Once it's sizzling, rest the kippers in, skin-side down. Set a weight on them to stop them curling up, so a fish weight or slightly smaller pan rested on top will do it (page 75). Fry for a couple of minutes to crisp up the skin before flipping and frying the flesh side.

Serve the herrings with the farls, split open and buttered generously, with the egg on top. A sprinkle of chives will add a little freshness.

To serve
4 very fresh eggs, to poach
plenty of butter for the farls
a few chives, snipped (optional)

Old-school yellow smoked haddock

The smoked haddock of my childhood was always, always luminescent yellow and with this recipe I wanted to honour that nostalgia. This one is coloured rather magically by just a little ground turmeric. It pleases me immensely that it's so bright, not to mention the health bonus turmeric brings, but it doesn't really impart any flavour so just leave it out if you'd rather a pale smoky fish.

As mentioned in the chapter intro, curing and smoking in the modern era need not be about preserving for longevity, so this uses rather less salt than is traditional. Once smoked, use within 3 days or freeze, well wrapped, for up to 3 months. The resulting fish is still pretty salty though, so you probably won't need to add any more when you cook it. The recipe is followed by two of my favourite smoked haddock recipes: fish pie (page 166) and the fishcakes (page 169) but it's also fab pan-fried with simple poached eggs on toast.

Pick a dish that fits the fish in a single snug layer and lay the fish skin-side up.

Mix the salt, sugar and turmeric in a small bowl, scrunching up the salt flakes a little as you go – wear gloves if you are bothered about yellow paws! Sprinkle a little – no more than a quarter, of the cure mix on the skin side of the fish and rub well in. Turn the fish over and sprinkle the rest on the flesh side, seasoning a little heavier towards the fat end and lighter towards the tail end. Slide into the fridge and leave to cure for 12 hours.

Rinse off the cure under running water and pat well dry with paper towel. Rest skin-side down on a rack hung over a tray and slide back into the fridge for another 6–12 hours to dry and develop a sticky pellicle.

Smoke in exactly the same way as the smoked trout (page 148), then remove, wrap in greaseproof (waxed) paper and chill for a few hours before cooking.

Serves 4

2 x 450–500g (1lb–2oz) haddock
   fillets, skin on
2 heaped tbsp flaked sea salt
2 tsp caster (superfine) sugar
1 tsp ground turmeric

Smoked fish pie with samphire and herbs

Fish pie is one of my ultimate comfort foods, it's such a cheering treat at any time of year and definitely not just relegated to winter in our house. I've given instructions here for baking in a conventional fan oven, but yes, I do like to make this on my barbecue too! To turn a barbecue into an 'oven' you need a high heat but an indirect one, so head back to pages 28–31 for heat and fire chat. If you have any little trimmings in the freezer saved from slicing your cured trout (see page 149), this is an excellent time to use them.

Set a saucepan on the hob over a low heat, add the butter and allow to melt. Tip in the onion and cook very gently for a good 20–30 minutes until really soft and translucent but not coloured.

Meanwhile, peel the potatoes for the mash and chop into large chunks. Add to a pan of lightly salted cold water and bring to the boil, then simmer for about 20 minutes until tender. Drain well, then mash until smooth. Beat with the butter and milk, seasoning with pepper but no extra salt. Set aside.

While the potatoes are cooking, set a deep frying pan on the hob over a medium heat and pour in the milk. Cut the fish, if necessary, to fit the pan in a single layer, then add it to the pan, skin-side down. Sprinkle over the mace and season really generously with black pepper but no salt as the fish will be salty enough. Cover with a lid or piece of foil and bring to the boil, then reduce the heat to a simmer and cook for 5 minutes. Turn off the heat and leave to rest for 10 minutes before lifting the fish onto a plate using a fish slice and set aside until cool enough to handle. Use your fingers to flake into large chucks, discarding the skin and any bones that you find. Reserve the milk for the sauce.

Preheat the oven to 180°C fan (200°C/400°F/gas 6). You could always bake the fish pie in a barbecue if you wanted to get outside – see page 23 for how to turn your barbecue into an oven; it's really very simple once you know how.

Serves 4

60g (2oz) butter
1 onion, finely chopped
600ml (20fl oz/2½ cups) milk
750g (1lb 10oz) smoked haddock
    (or a mix of haddock plus any
    smoked fish trimmings you
    may have)
a good pinch of ground mace
50g (2oz) plain (all-purpose) flour
a handful of samphire, about
    75g (2½oz)
a good handful of soft fresh herbs
    (such as tarragon, parsley,
    chives, dill), about 25g (¾oz)
freshly ground black pepper

For the mash

1.2kg (2lb 10oz) floury potatoes
50g (2oz) butter
50–75ml (3½–5 tbsp) milk
freshly ground black pepper
150g (5oz) mature Cheddar
    (maybe home smoked,
    see page 147)

Once the onion is soft, stir through the flour, cooking it over a gentle heat for a minute or so until it is combined. Pour in the reserved warm milk, whisking constantly until the sauce is smooth and glossy. Turn up the heat a little and bring to the boil, then cook for a good 5 minutes to cook the flour, stirring frequently. Add the samphire and herbs and stir together, then turn off the heat and gently fold through the fish flakes. Pour into a deep ovenproof dish.

Spoon the mashed potato to completely cover the sauce, ruffling up the top with the tines of a fork. Sprinkle on the Cheddar and slide the dish into the oven, or take to the barbecue, and bake for about 25–30 minutes until golden and crispy.

Classic fishcakes

A classic leftovers recipe in our house and a great way to turn a little fish into another whole meal. I make them most often with leftover smoked or cured fish, which is why they find their way into this chapter, but to be honest any fish would be great. I guess the fuller the flavour of the fish, the more tasty the fishcakes will be, but I would argue that the greatness of your fishcakes also lies in the quality of your mash so make sure it has enough butter, milk and seasoning for it to be delicious in its own right. If you have made plenty for your fish pie, you may have enough left over. Otherwise, you'll need to start by making a fresh batch of mash.

Put the mash in a mixing bowl and add the spring onions, parsley and horseradish sauce and a generous grind of salt and pepper and mix together really well.

Flake the fish with your fingers, discarding any skin and bones. Add the flakes to the mash mixture and fold together until combined, but don't overmix so the flakes don't get too broken up. Divide into 8 evenly sized balls and pat out between your palms to about 2cm (¾in) thick discs. Set on a tray. At this point you can slide them into the fridge and leave until you are ready to cook – loosely covered, they will keep for a couple of days.

To make the dressing, put the vinegar, mustard and honey into a bowl and whisk together. Add the dill and season well with salt and pepper. Gradually drizzle in the olive oil, whisking constantly as you go until it is emulsified. Set aside.

When you are ready to cook, line up 3 shallow bowls: one with the flour, one with the eggs and one with the breadcrumbs. Add a pinch of salt to the eggs and whisk with a fork – the salt will thin the egg a little and make it better at coating the fishcakes.

Take one fishcake and gently toss it in the flour to coat all over, then add to the egg and do the same. Finally dip it into the breadcrumbs and roll it around so it gets completely covered before setting it back on the tray. Repeat with the other fishcakes.

Pour a couple of millimetres of oil into a frying pan and set over a medium–high heat on the hob. Drop a breadcrumb into the oil to test how hot it is; the crumb should sizzle to golden in a few seconds. Once it is hot enough, add the fishcakes – cooking in a couple of batches if necessary – and fry until deeply golden brown, about 4 minutes or so. Flip over and cook the other side.

Give the sauce a quick whisk up and pour into a serving bowl. Serve alongside the fishcakes.

Makes 8 fishcakes, to serve 4

700g (1lb 9oz) cold mashed potato (see page 166)
1 bunch of spring onions (scallions), finely chopped
a small handful of flat-leaf parsley, chopped
2–3 tbsp horseradish sauce, to taste
300–330g (10½–11oz) cooked fish, such as smoked haddock, cured trout or a combination of bits and bobs
50g (2oz/heaped ⅓ cup) plain (all-purpose) flour
2 eggs
150g (5oz/3 cups) fresh breadcrumbs
olive oil, for shallow frying
flaked sea salt and freshly ground black pepper

For the mustard dill sauce

4 tbsp white wine vinegar
2 generous tbsp wholegrain or Dijon mustard
2 tbsp runny honey
a small bunch of fresh dill, chopped, about 25g (¾oz)
6 tbsp extra virgin olive oil

SALT COD

Preservation by drying and salting is an ancient technique deployed the world over. This recipe is borderline chapter-inappropriate as it is not smoked. But it is cured way beyond all other fish in the book, so I slid it in.

Once dried, you then need to soak to reconstitute and remove the salt before you can cook and eat it, which may naturally and sensibly lead you to the question of why you would bother to do it in the first place. The dehydration and salting process disrupts cell structure, alters texture and intensifies flavour molecules so even after rehydrating you are left with a fish that both tastes and feels different in your mouth than fresh cod.

How to make salt cod

I live in a city with relatively easy access to salt cod, thanks to a sizeable Caribbean community but generally it can be a little hard to find. The good news is it is very easy to make; all you need is fish, salt and time. You can prepare any low-fat white fish in this way – haddock, ling, hake, pollack – all take well to this salting and drying process. Oily fish, like mackerel, herring or salmon aren't great with this technique as the fats tend to go rancid over time.

You will lose about 50% weight after the salting and drying is complete. This quantity below makes enough to cook one batch each of the Salt cod brandade stuffed peppers (page 172) and the Celeriac and salt cod rosti (page 185).

800–900g (1lb 12oz–2lb) fillet of cod, skin on
an equal weight of fine sea salt

Choose a dish that will fit the fish in a single, snug layer and sprinkle a deep bed of salt, about 1cm (½in) over the bottom. Rest the fish on top, skin-side down, pushing it down so the skin gets complete contact with the salt. Sprinkle the rest of the salt over the top, again a good 1cm (½in) deep, making sure the fish is completely and generously covered. Slide into the fridge and leave undisturbed for 48 hours.

After 48 hours remove the fillet and wash off the salt under cold running water. Pat really dry with paper towels, then rest skin-side down on a rack hung over a tray. Slide in the fridge and leave to dry out for 7–10 days. If you have thin muslin cloth (cheesecloth) you can wrap it lightly, but I tend to dry it uncovered. After the drying time, wrap tightly in baking parchment and slide into an airtight box or bag. The cod will keep happily for months if not longer – this preservation method predates refrigeration by a long way, but I generally store it in the fridge out of modern habit.

When you are ready to cook the cod, you will need to soak it in cold water for at least 24 hours in the fridge, changing the water a few times to rehydrate and rinse out some of the salt.

Salt cod brandade stuffed peppers

I make this in a food mixer using the paddle attachment to beat it to a paste. You can also use a food processor, but the texture will be smoother, or do it the traditional way by pounding a pestle and mortar. Stuffing things is always tricky on the size front, so you may need to adjust the quantities up or down to fit the size of what you are filling.

Take a large, deep frying pan and lay in the cod, cutting it into pieces so it fits in a single layer. Cover well with cold water and set over a medium heat on the hob. Tuck in the bay leaves and garlic cloves, season well with black pepper and cover loosely with a lid. Bring up to the boil and simmer for 5 minutes. Turn off the heat and leave to rest for another 10 minutes.

Lift the cod to a plate and leave to cool a little until it's comfortable to touch. Scoop the garlic cloves out of the cooking water and add to the bowl of a freestanding food mixer. Flake the fish into the mixer bowl and discard the skin, taking care to remove any little bones you find as you go. Add the parsley and a really generous grind of black pepper and set the mixer going to beat the fish to a paste. With the motor running, drizzle in the extra virgin olive oil in a thin stream until it is emulsified into the fish and you have a creamy paste. Add the mashed potato, black olives and sherry vinegar and mix until combined.

Slice the peppers in half lengthways and use a teaspoon to scoop out the seeds and membranes. Spoon the brandade into the halves, pressing it in so it gets into all the cracks and crevices. Once stuffed, they will keep for a couple of days in the fridge.

When you are ready to cook, fire up your barbecue ready for direct and indirect cooking (page 31).

Set a small pan on the hob over a medium heat and add the breadcrumbs and olive oil. Toast for a few minutes until golden and crispy, then sprinkle over the top of the stuffed peppers.

Slide the peppers onto a grill tray and set onto the grill bars a little away from the fire. Cook for about 15 minutes or until the peppers are starting to soften, rotating the tray halfway so that each side gets even access to the heat source. Once soft you can slide the tray over the heat to roast the peppers until they are lightly charred and soft all the way through.

Scatter with parsley and drizzle with olive oil before serving.

Serves 2–3, depending on what else you are eating

400–450g (14–16oz) dried salt cod, soaked in cold water for 24 hours (see previous page)
3 bay leaves
3 garlic cloves
a good handful of flat-leaf parsley, about 15g (½oz), chopped
100ml (3½fl oz/scant ½ cup) extra virgin olive oil
200g (7oz) cold mashed potato (page 166)
50g (2oz) black olives, chopped
2 tbsp sherry vinegar
3 long Romano peppers or about 12 sweet baby peppers
50g (2oz/1 cup) fresh breadcrumbs
2 tbsp olive oil
freshly ground black pepper

To serve
a little extra parsley
a drizzle of your best extra virgin olive oil

Chapter 5: Burgers and fritters

What's a barbecue without stuff you eat out of your hand or with a fork at most? Relaxed eating, a little messy, no standing on ceremony, just tasty stuff to eat. That's not to say these recipes are necessarily quick or simple – even casual eating sometimes needs time to build the best flavours.

My strategy when faced with a recipe that seems at first glance a touch long-winded is to break it into steps so you can spread the work load and I have tried to give you guidance within the methods. So, for example, in this chapter, make the tortilla dough for the tacos a good couple of hours ahead of cooking, along with the slaws. With the hotdogs, you can spread the steps over a good 36 hours, or the fishage rolls can even be frozen uncooked for 3 months.

Once you've broken down the prep stages into parts, the cooking becomes pretty quick and the eating, more importantly, is effortless.

Garam masala spiced fish naan

Naan bread bakes very well directly on the grill bars over a fairly hot but indirect heat. Here the raw dough is stuffed with spiced mackerel fillets that cook as the bread is baking to create a delicious hot fish sandwich. In this recipe, the fish skin doesn't get crisp as it is inside the naan so you could try and remove it if you prefer (page 20). However, they have thin skin so it's not the easiest of jobs, and I tend to not bother as the skin is full of good nutrients.

For the dough, weigh the flour into a mixing bowl and stir through the yeast and salt. Put the boiling water into a jug, then spoon in the yogurt, stirring it together until combined, then pour into the flour. Stir together to get a rough, shaggy ball of dough, then tip onto a lightly oiled worktop. Knead gently for a few minutes until smooth, then chop into 4 even-sized pieces, shaping each into a ball by cupping in one palm and smoothing the surface with the other. Rest on a lightly oiled baking sheet and loosely cover with a clean dish towel. Leave to prove until doubled in size, about 1–2 hours, depending on the warmth of the room.

Meanwhile, put the onion slivers in a small bowl with a sprinkle of salt and the lime juice. Use your hands to massage together a little to soften the onion. Set aside.

Set a small frying pan over a medium heat on the hob and tip in the cardamon, coriander and cumin seeds, the peppercorns, fennel seeds, cloves and crumbled cinnamon. Toast for a couple of minutes before tipping into a pestle and mortar or a spice mill. Add a teaspoon of salt and grind to a powder.

Lay the mackerel fillets out in a single layer in a baking pan and sprinkle the spice powder all over, patting it down so it sticks. Slide into the fridge for an hour or so while the dough rises.

Serves 4

1 small red onion, very
    thinly sliced
juice of 1 lime
8 cardamon pods, bruised open
    and seeds picked out
2 tbsp coriander seeds
1 tbsp cumin seeds
1 tsp black peppercorns
1 tsp fennel seeds
½ tsp cloves
½ cinnamon stick, crumbled
    (about 1 tsp)
4 mackerel, about 250g (9oz)
    each, filleted, or 8 fillets
4 tbsp mango chutney
a loose handful of coriander
    (cilantro), about 25g (¾oz),
    chopped
flaked sea salt

For the dough

300g (10½oz/2½ cups) strong
    white bread flour, plus extra
    for shaping
1 tsp fast-action yeast
½ tsp flaked sea salt
75ml (5 tbsp) boiling water
150g (5oz/scant ⅔ cup) full-fat
    yogurt
a little vegetable oil, to drizzle

Make the sauce by mixing together all the yogurt sauce ingredients in a bowl. Refrigerate until needed.

Once the dough has proved, lightly sprinkle the worktop with flour. Take a ball and pat it out to a circle about 5–7mm (¼in) thick. Make sure it's not stuck to the worktop and add a little more flour underneath, if necessary, then rest one fillet skin-side down onto one side of the dough circle. It doesn't matter that the fish may be a little bigger than the dough, those bits will get crispy! Lightly flour a baking pan.

Spread a tablespoon of mango chutney over the fillet and top with a quarter of the onions and a sprinkle of coriander before laying another fillet on top to make a sandwich. Fold up the other side of the dough, crimping a little to make a seal along the edge, like a Cornish pasty, then transfer to the prepared baking pan. Repeat with the other 3 balls of dough. At this point you can slide the tray into the fridge for a couple of hours if you like.

When you are ready to cook, light the barbecue. I like to have a fire in the middle of mine, with a fire-free ring around the outside edge (page 31) so that each mackerel naan is equidistant from the heat source. Moderate the air vents so you have a temperature on the lid of around 170°C (338°F).

Brush the grill bars really clean with a wire brush. Rest the naan on the bars away from the fire and shut the lid. Cook for about 5 minutes each side, or until the dough is crisp and the fish is cooked through, rotating halfway so they cook evenly – a probe pierced deep into the centre should read 60°C (140°F). If the dough is cooked but the fish is not quite, shut the vents down more to lower the heat and continue cooking until they are done.

Serve hot or warm with the yogurt sauce on the side.

For the yogurt sauce
300g (10½oz/scant 1¼ cups)
    Greek yogurt
3 tbsp chopped mint leaves
juice of ½ lemon
2 garlic cloves, crushed to a paste
flaked sea salt and freshly ground
    black pepper

TWO FISH TACOS

A corn tortilla is such a perfect vessel for grilled fish I've included two recipes here, one with mackerel and one with ray. The method for making tortillas is identical for both versions, so in the interest of avoiding repetition, I've abbreviated the instructions in the second recipe, so do refer back for more detail if you need to. It goes without saying, if you're not feeling a tortilla-making vibe, grab some from the shop. And actually, both fillings would be just grand shoved in a bun with the trimmings, in a burger-meets-taco mash-up.

Blackened mackerel tacos with gooseberry salsa

Mackerel really is one of the best fish we could be eating: sustainable, really good for us and, thanks to the oil-rich flesh, dead easy to cook on a barbecue. Here it's coated in a Mexican spice rub before being grilled until crispy and stuffed into tacos. The gooseberry salsa is good and sharp, the perfect foil to the mackerel's richness, but I know they are not the easiest things to source; a lime-juice-rich tomato salsa would work well. As an aside, if you have a spare corner in your garden, a gooseberry bush is a lovely low-maintenance way to fill it.

Four to six hours before you want to cook, lay the mackerel fillets, skin-side up, on a rack hung over a tray and slide into the fridge so the skin can dry. Once again, this is an important step to minimize sticking (page 26).

A couple of hours before you want to cook, make the fish spice rub by stirring together the garlic, cumin, paprika, chilli, oil, brown sugar and salt in a small bowl. Spread all over the mackerel and slide back into the fridge to marinate.

At the same time, weigh the masa harina into a mixing bowl and stir through the salt. Pour in the warm water and mix. Once it has come together as a ball, tip onto the worktop and knead briefly for a minute or so. Wrap in clingfilm (plastic wrap) or baking parchment and set aside at room temperature to rest. I always find it is easy to press or roll after a good couple of hours' rest.

Make the slaw by mixing together the cabbage and a good sprinkle of salt, using clean hands to massage the salt in to soften the cabbage (so it's easier to eat). Add the red pepper and spring onions and stir through along with the olive oil and red wine vinegar to taste, then season well with pepper. Set aside. It will be happy in the fridge for 24 hours.

Makes 12 tacos, to serve 4–6

3 mackerel, filleted
3 garlic cloves, crushed to a paste
2 tbsp cumin seeds, toasted and ground
1–2 tbsp hot smoked paprika, to taste
1–2 tsp chilli powder, to taste
3 tbsp olive oil
1 tbsp brown sugar
1 heaped tbsp flaked sea salt

For the corn tortillas

300g (10½oz/scant 2½ cups) masa harina
1 tbsp flaked sea salt
400ml (13fl oz/generous 1½ cups) warm water (half boiling mixed with half cold)

Fire up the barbecue ready for direct grilling, setting a large frying pan over the fire to heat up ready for cooking the tortillas. You can also cook them on the hob inside if you prefer.

Divide the dough into 12 equal pieces, shaping each into a ball. If you have one, use a tortilla press lined with a sheet of greaseproof (waxed) paper or clingfilm (plastic wrap) to press into discs of around 3mm (¼in) thick. If you don't have a press, you can hand shape with a rolling pin between 2 sheets of greaseproof paper.

Lift a tortilla onto the hot pan, taking a little care as they are fragile when uncooked – I find it best to peel off one side of the paper, invert it onto the hot surface, then peel away the other piece. Cook for 1–2 minutes on one side, then flip over and cook on the other. Wrap in foil or a clean dish towel to keep warm and pliable and repeat with the rest of the dough. With practice, and depending on the size of your pan, you may be able to get in a rhythm of pressing and cooking several at once.

Once all the tortillas are cooked and wrapped, set a grill tray over the fire to get hot and onto that rest a flameproof frying pan.

Pour the tablespoon of olive oil into the frying pan and tip in the gooseberries. Stir through the chilli and sugar, shut the lid of the barbecue and leave for around 10–15 minutes or until the gooseberries have collapsed. Stir through the coriander and taste to check for sourness – you may want to add a little more sugar to taste. Scoop into a bowl ready for serving.

Make sure the fire and the grill tray are both hot now; add a little more fuel if you need to and remove the lid of the barbecue to let the oxygen flow freely (pages 28–31). Rest the fish on the grill tray, skin-side down and set a fish weight or pan on top of them to stop them curling up. Grill for just 2–3 minutes until the skin is crisp. Use a fish slice to tease off the grill tray, flip over and cook for just a minute or so on the flesh side.

To serve, cut the mackerel into chunky slices. Spoon a little slaw into a tortilla and top with a slice or two of fish. Add a spoon of the gooseberry salsa, a little dollop of sour cream and a sprinkle of coriander before tucking in.

For the slaw
½ small white or green cabbage, about 400g (14oz), finely sliced
1 red pepper, thinly sliced
3 spring onions (scallions), finely sliced
5 tbsp extra virgin olive oil
2–3 tbsp red wine vinegar, to taste
flaked sea salt and freshly ground black pepper

For the gooseberry salsa
1 tbsp olive oil
500g (1lb 2oz) gooseberries, topped and tailed
5 green chillies (fresh jalapeño if you can get them), or to taste, thinly sliced
2 tbsp sugar, or to taste
a handful of coriander (cilantro), chopped

To serve
a few tbsp sour cream
a little extra coriander (cilantro)

Pulled ray tacos with salsa macha

I've specified ray here over skate as a deliberate effort to big up ray as a better choice, although you're likely to still see it labelled as skate in the fishmongers even if it isn't. Confused? Return to pages 8–10 for a little tale of fish sustainability. Whatever we call it, it's a fabulous treat on the barbecue and rather conveniently it gently 'pulls' into nice little strands, much like pulled pork, making it an excellent taco filling.

Salsa macha, one of my favourite sauces, is a chilli, peanut and sesame-laden oil that is spicy, crunchy and completely addictive. This recipe makes plenty, a good couple of jam jars, as it stores for a generous 6–8 weeks in the fridge and it goes with loads of stuff – a fried egg sarnie being my personal favourite, or dolloped on roast chicken or grilled veggies, or over fried rice. Guajillo chillies are earthy and fruity, whereas Ancho are slightly smoky, with almost a chocolatey rich smell. Both can be found easily online, along with the masa harina. Neither are particularly fiery so I add a little regular dried chilli (hot pepper) flakes from a supermarket jar to boost the heat.

You can make the salsa macha up to 6–8 weeks in advance. Pour the oil into a small heavy-based saucepan and set over a medium heat on the hob. Have a large dessert bowl and a slotted spoon handy. Once the oil is warm, drop in the garlic cloves and fry gently for a few minutes until they are a shade or two darker, taking care not to burn them. Remove with a slotted spoon and drop into the bowl. Add the Guajillo chilli pieces and fry for a minute, before removing to the bowl with the slotted spoon, then repeat with the Ancho pieces, again frying for just a minute before removing. Drop the peanuts into the oil and fry for a little longer, maybe 4–5 minutes, until they are deeply golden, adding the sesame seed and chilli flakes for the last couple of minutes. Slide off the heat and allow to cool for 15 minutes before pouring the lot into a food processor. Add the fried garlic and chillies back in, along with the vinegar, sugar and salt. Blitz until roughly chopped – don't overdo it, a good bit of texture is welcome. Scoop into clean jars, seal and store in the fridge.

A couple of hours before you want to cook, make the tortilla dough in exactly the same way as in the previous recipe.

Makes 12 tacos, to serve 4–6

For the salsa macha
500ml (17fl oz/2 cups) olive oil
6 whole garlic cloves, peeled
6 Guajillo chillies, stems removed, sliced into 1cm (½in) pieces
4 Ancho chillies, stems removed, sliced into 1cm (½in) pieces
200g (7oz/1¼ cups) roasted peanuts
3 tbsp sesame seeds
1–2 tbsp regular dried chilli (hot pepper) flakes, to up the heat to taste
2 tbsp white wine vinegar
1 tbsp light soft brown sugar
1 tbsp flaked sea salt

For the corn tortillas
300g (10½oz/scant 2½ cups) masa harina
1 tbsp flaked sea salt
400ml (13fl oz/generous 1½ cups) warm water (half boiling mixed with half cold)

At the same time, make the slaw by stirring together the cabbage, sugar and salt in a bowl, using clean hands to massage the cabbage so it softens a little, making it more flexible (and so easier to eat!). Add the tomatoes, spring onions and half the coriander, saving the rest for garnish. Stir through the lime juice, season well with black pepper and set aside.

Fire up the barbecue ready for direct grilling (page 31). At this point you can roll and cook the tortillas in exactly the same way as in the previous recipe (see page 180), then continue with the fish. Once all the tortillas are cooked and wrapped, set a grill tray or fish cage over the fire to get hot.

Rest the ray on a tray and drizzle with the olive oil, rubbing it all over. Stir the flour and ground cumin seeds together in a small bowl, along with a good grind of salt and pepper. Sprinkle all over both sides of the wings and rub in well.

Lift the wings onto the hot fish cage or grill tray and cook for a few minutes on each side until crisp and lightly charred in places, and a probe reads around 55°C (131°F) in the deepest part. Remove and leave to rest for a few minutes to finish bringing the temperature up to 60°C (140°F).

To serve, use two forks to shred the meat off the ray wings. Spoon a little slaw into the centre of a tortilla, top with a little fish and a good drizzle of the salsa macha. Finish with a sprinkle of the reserved coriander and tuck in.

For the slaw

400g (14oz) red cabbage, finely shredded
1 tsp caster (superfine) sugar, to taste
½ tsp flaked sea salt
150g (5oz) cherry tomatoes, finely chopped
4 spring onions (scallions), finely sliced
1 garlic clove, crushed
a bunch of coriander (cilantro), chopped (about 20g/¾oz)
juice of 2 limes
freshly ground black pepper

For the ray

800g (1lb 12oz) ray wings – thornback is often a great choice
1 tbsp olive oil
2 tbsp plain (all-purpose) flour
2 tbsp cumin seeds, ground
flaked sea salt and freshly ground black pepper

TWO FISH FRITTERS

The following two recipes are a great way of taking a little fish and making it go further, saving pennies and conserving precious fish resources while you're at it. Beyond that ... what you've got here is fried crispy things with bags of flavour. You could just as easily cook both these in a frying pan on your hob, but in keeping with my personal ethos on fire cooking, if the sun is shining and the birds are chirping, then cooking outside is one of the most positive ways I can choose to live my life.

Smoked fish and courgette pancakes with avocado salad

A deliciously easy brunch dish designed to use a couple of handfuls of fish trimmings that you might just have squirrelled away in the freezer after trying some of the smoking recipes. To be honest, I would buy fish just for these, and actually any fish would do. I just feel like smoky fish fits for brunch. The gram flour is also optional; you could easily sub in regular plain (all-purpose) flour but gram flour is made of chickpeas and is such an easy win to boost protein and other nutrients in your diet. Find it in many supermarkets and, of course, online.

Tip the grated courgette into a sieve hung over a bowl and sprinkle on the salt. Use your hands to give it a quick mix together, then set a saucer on top and rest a weight onto it – a tin or two of beans is ideal – and leave aside for 30 minutes.

Make the salad by stirring the avocados, tomatoes, basil and lemon juice in a bowl. Season with a little salt and pepper.

Once the courgette has drained, discard the water from the bowl and tip in the courgette. Add the fish, yogurt, eggs, flour, bicarbonate of soda and black pepper and stir together.

Fire up the barbecue ready for direct grilling (page 31); you won't need a great deal of charcoal as these are pretty speedy to cook.

Serves 4

2 courgettes (zucchini), grated
1 tsp flaked sea salt
250g (9oz) smoked fish trimmings, chopped into 1cm (½in) snippets
200g (7oz/scant 1 cup) full-fat Greek yogurt
2 eggs
150g (5oz/heaped 1⅓ cups) gram flour
1 tsp bicarbonate of soda (baking soda)
a good drizzle of olive oil, to cook

Once hot, set a frying pan directly over the fire (or indeed over a medium-high heat on your hob if you prefer) and drizzle in some olive oil. Dollop tablespoons of the pancake mixture round the pan, spacing them out a little as they will puff up as they cook.

Cook for a couple of minutes on each side until golden brown and cooked through. Depending on the size of your cooking surface, you will probably need to do this in 2–3 batches, keeping them warm on a plate as you go.

Serve the pancakes on warmed plates with a little of the avocado salad dolloped on top.

For the avocado salad
2 avocados, chopped
150g (5oz) ripe cherry tomatoes, chopped
a handful of basil leaves
juice of 1 lemon
flaked sea salt and freshly ground black pepper

Celeriac and salt cod rosti with burnt apple mayo

The cod needs soaking in cold water for 48 hours before using here, as per the method on page 170.

Salty and crunchy, these rosti are best eaten fresh out of the pan while still tongue-burningly hot, so I would make a batch, eat it, share it, and then make another batch before repeating. If celeriac isn't your thing, or you can't get hold of it, this would work equally well with grated potatoes or even parsnips.

The apple mayo is a revelation, so do give it a go even if you think it sounds a bit weird. If you are making these on your hob inside, just add a slight drizzle of oil to the apple wedges and fry in a hot pan to get a bit of caramelized colour into them.

To cook the cod, take a large, deep frying pan and lay in the fish, cutting it into pieces so it fits in a single layer. Cover well with cold water and set over a medium heat. Tuck in the bay leaves and garlic cloves, season well with black pepper and cover loosely with a lid. Bring up to the boil, then simmer for 5 minutes. Turn off the heat and leave to rest, still covered, for another 10 minutes.

Use a fish slice to lift the fish onto a plate. Once the fish is cool enough to handle, use your fingers to pull it into flakes, discarding the skin and any little bones you find. Transfer to a clean plate as you go.

Squeeze the lemon juice into a mixing bowl. Peel and coarsely grate the celeriac and drop into the lemon juice. Use your hands to mix and massage them together; the juice will stop the celeriac from browning. Add the eggs, flour, mustard and sage. Season well with black pepper and stir through the flaked salt cod. Set aside. The mixture will happily keep in the fridge for a few hours if you want to get ahead.

Serves 4

400–450g (14–16oz) dry weight salt cod (soaked and rehydrated as on page 170)
3 bay leaves
3 garlic cloves, peeled and bruised open
juice of 1 lemon
500–600g (1lb 2oz–1lb 5oz) celeriac
2 eggs
75g (2½oz/scant ⅔ cup) plain (all-purpose) flour
2 tbsp English mustard
a loose handful fresh sage leaves, finely chopped (about 10g/⅓oz)
olive oil, for shallow frying
freshly ground black pepper

When you are ready to cook, fire up your barbecue ready for direct grilling but, as always, leaving a zone on your barbecue fuel free so you have heat control (page 31).

While the barbecue is heating up, quarter the apples and remove the cores. Take to the grill and rest over the fire; setting them on a grill tray is a great idea if you have one so you don't need to worry about the apples falling through the grill bars. Cook over the heat for a few minutes to caramelize and soften them, sliding them slightly away from the heat if they colour too quickly. Remove and allow to go cold before very finely chopping and dropping into a small mixing bowl. Stir through the mayonnaise and capers and season to taste with freshly ground black pepper. Set aside.

Set a large frying pan on the grill bars over the fire and pour in a generous glug of olive oil, enough to coat the base of the pan with a millimetre or two. Once hot, dollop in tablespoons of the rosti mix and fry for 3–4 minutes until golden and crispy. Flip over with a fish slice and cook on the other side.

Once cooked, drain on a plate lined with paper towel for a minute or so before spooning a dollop of the burnt apple mayo onto each. Sprinkle with a few snipped chives and tuck in while hot. Repeat until you have used all the mixture.

For the burnt apple mayo

4 small eating apples, about 500g (1lb 2oz)
100g (3½oz/scant ½ cup) mayonnaise
2 tbsp capers
a handful of chives, snipped, to garnish
freshly ground black pepper

Hake burgers, grilled aubergine and membrillo tomato chutney

Hake has a good sturdy texture that is great as a burger – think of these as giant fish fingers in a bun – but you could use any chunky white fish here. They are best cooked in a pan over the fire as you want a good amount of oil to get the all-important crispy breadcrumbs.

I love membrillo, a tart sticky paste made from slow-cooked quinces. Normally served alongside cheese, here it adds a sweet and sour note to the chutney. It's pretty easy to find these days, definitely online, or make friends with someone (me, me!) who has a quince tree, as they are likely to have a tonne of the stuff.

For the chutney, set a small saucepan on the hob over a medium heat and pour in the olive oil. Add the tomatoes, garlic and chilli flakes, if using, and cook for a few minutes until the tomatoes have collapsed. Add the membrillo and sherry vinegar and season with a little salt and pepper. Cook for another few minutes, stirring until the membrillo has dissolved, then remove from the heat, scoop into a bowl and set aside to cool.

When you are ready to cook, fire up the barbecue ready for direct grilling (page 31).

Tip the breadcrumbs into a bowl and stir through the smoked paprika and a generous grind of salt and pepper. Crack the egg into another bowl and lightly beat with a fork. Add the flour to a third bowl.

Toss the fillets about in the flour to coat all over, then dip into the egg until evenly covered. Add to the bowl of breadcrumbs and flip over a couple of times so each one is evenly coated in crumbs. Line up on a plate. If your hands get unbearably messy, stop, wash and begin again.

Serves 4

140g (4¾oz/3 cups) breadcrumbs
2 tsp hot smoked paprika
1 egg
3 tbsp plain (all-purpose) flour
4 x 125g (4oz) hake fillets
1 aubergine (eggplant), cut into
    1cm (½in) slices
olive oil, to fry and grill

For the spiced tomato chutney

2 tbsp olive oil
200g (7oz) cherry tomatoes,
    quartered
2 garlic cloves, thinly sliced
a pinch of chilli (hot pepper)
    flakes (optional)
50g (2oz) membrillo
2 tsp sherry vinegar
flaked sea salt and freshly ground
    black pepper

To serve

a good handful of rocket (arugula)
4 ciabatta buns

Drizzle a little olive oil over the aubergine slices and season with salt and pepper. Set on the grill bars over the fire and grill until lightly charred all over. Slide away from the fire so they keep warm and set a flameproof frying pan over the fire to heat up. Pour in a good amount of olive oil so it coats the pan by a couple of millimetres.

Once the oil is hot, add the crumbed fish and fry for a couple of minutes on each side until crisp and golden. Use a temperature probe to test the fish for doneness – it should be 60°C (140°F) deep in the centre. Slide the pan off the heat a little if the crumbs are colouring too quickly so the fish can finish cooking. Once the fish is done, split the buns open and toast briefly on the cut side.

To serve, add a little rocket to the base of each bun, then add the fish and a couple of slices of aubergine. Finish with a dollop of the chutney, top with the bun lid and tuck in.

Smoked fish hotdogs with cucumber pickles and crispy onions

Yes indeed, making a fish hotdog, just as with any sausage, is something of a labour of love. It's certainly not something I would do regularly but on occasion it's ridiculously satisfying and very tasty. You can break it down into a couple of steps over a couple of days and it then becomes pretty straightforward. So I would tend to treat it as a bit of a weekend project, grinding and mixing on Friday evening, chilling overnight, then stuffing and drying the following morning, finally smoking ready in time for Saturday tea. They also freeze really well, tightly wrapped, unsmoked. So if you're in a sausage-making mood, make double and freeze some. They will keep for 3 months and you can smoke them from frozen.

You can mince the mix in a food processor if you don't have a mincer, but you will need a sausage stuffer to fill the casings. If you don't have one, consider making the mix and frying in a pan like little burgers or fritters. It won't be a smoky dog but it will taste good!

The drying step is important as it will help give you that satisfying 'snap' when you bite into it. These are made with traditional hog casings; you can certainly use collagen cases for a pescatarian version but they are slightly trickier to work with and don't quite bite the same.

Check that your trout is free of pin bones and remove with fish tweezers, and if it's still skin on, remove that too (page 20). Cut into 1cm (½in) slices, dropping into a mixing bowl as you go. Add the prawns, leek, crème fraîche, breadcrumbs, mustard, smoked paprika, mace, salt and pepper. Stir together really well.

Then you have two options. You can blitz the mixture in a food processor so it comes together as a thick purée, or you can grind it in a mincer if you have one. I use my mincer and send the mixture through twice for a fine grind. At this point you can refrigerate the mix overnight if you like.

When you are ready to stuff, set up your sausage stuffer, packing the mixer down well into the compartment to minimize air gaps. Drain the casings, find the end and feed onto the nozzle. Set a slightly wet tray underneath the stuffer nozzle so the hotdogs slide across it as they come out the machine. Fill the casings, taking care not to over-stuff or they can split, and when they are all full, twist into links. They shrink a little on cooking so link just a little longer than the length of your buns. Rest on a rack over a tray and slide into the fridge, uncovered, to dry out for a good few hours – 4–6 would be great if you have time, or up to 12.

Makes about 8–10 hotdogs

700g (1lb 9oz) trout fillet, skinless, boneless
150g (5oz) coldwater prawns (shrimp), drained of any liquid from the packaging
1 small leek, chopped (about 150g/5oz)
100g (3½oz/scant ½ cup) crème fraîche
60g (2oz/1¼ cups) fresh breadcrumbs
2 tbsp English mustard powder
1 tbsp smoked paprika
1 heaped tsp ground mace
1 heaped tbsp flaked sea salt
1 tbsp freshly ground black pepper
about 2–3 metres (yards) hog casings, soaked overnight in cold water

When you are ready to cook, fire up the barbecue with a small fire to one side and moderate your air vents to get a steady low temperature of around 120°C (248°F) – see pages 28–31 for fire tips. Add 2–3 lumps of smoking wood of your choice (page 139). Lay the hotdogs on the grill bars as far from the fire as you can get them so they smoke over a low indirect heat. Shut the lid and leave to cook for 3 hours or so, turning over once or twice during that time, and rotating if necessary so they all get an even-ish heat. The ones closer to the fire will obviously be getting a little hotter than those further away.

While the dogs are smoking, make the cucumber pickles by stirring together the cucumber strips with the salt in a sieve hung over a bowl. Set a small plate into the sieve with a weight, like a can of beans, on top. Leave for 20–30 minutes to drain away some of the water. Tip the cucumber into a clean bowl along with the gherkins, vinegar, crème fraîche and dill. Add a pinch of sugar to taste and season with salt and pepper.

Pour some vegetable oil into a deep, heavy-based frying pan and set over a high heat on the hob. Tip in the onions along with a generous pinch of salt and fry until deeply golden. Remove with a slotted spoon to a plate lined with a few layers of paper towel and leave to drain and crisp up. Set aside (out of reach as they are really very munch-able).

When the hotdogs are smoked to perfection – test the temperature with a probe after 3 hours; you want to ensure they are over 60°C (140°F) – remove them from the grill. Warm the buns a little over the heat, then slice down the top. Add a hotdog, followed by a little cucumber pickle. Squeeze over mustard to taste and sprinkle on the crispy onions.

For the cucumber pickles
½ cucumber, peeled into long
    strips with a veg peeler
    (discard the seedy centre)
1 tsp flaked sea salt
4 large gherkins, finely chopped
2 tbsp red wine vinegar
2 tbsp crème fraîche
20g (¾oz) dill, chopped
a pinch of caster (superfine)
    sugar, to taste

For the crispy onions
vegetable oil, for frying
3 large onions, finely sliced

To serve
hotdog buns, one per dog
mustard of your choice

Mackerel, leek and horseradish fishage rolls

Like a sausage roll but with fish, obvs. The addition of leek and chopped potato adds soft sweetness and also bulks out the filling, making a little fish go a long way. Don't worry about the amount of horseradish, its spiky heat tones down loads on cooking. You can easily prep the filling ahead of time as it will sit happily in the fridge for 24 hours or so. Or you could even fully prep the rolls and store in the fridge or freezer until you want to bake them. They can be baked from frozen.

And yes, you can bake on a barbecue! I do so often, both savoury stuff and cakes, simply because I know I can and it's really just another excuse for me to get outside where I am happiest. Whether you want to or not is your call, these would obviously work in your fan oven too. The trick to barbecue baking is to think 'oven' – you need to create a fairly high but indirect heat, relying on mostly convection currents to do the work for you. It is a bit of a leap of faith not to keep opening the lid of your barbecue to check it's cooking. My best tip? Use your nose – one of my favourite senses in fire cooking. A little sniff around the air vents will yield plenty of clues, and if you smell burning you know things are too hot or too direct. See pages 28–31 for fire and grill set-up details.

Remove the pastry from the fridge a good 30–45 minutes before you want to use it so it comes to room temperature. This will stop it cracking when you unroll it. If it's a crazy hot day, reduce this time a little.

Set a saucepan over a low heat on the hob and toss in the butter. As it melts, add the olive oil, followed by the leeks, potatoes, thyme leaves and a good grind of salt and pepper. Cook for a generous 15-20 minutes, stirring fairly often, until the leeks are melting and the potatoes soft. Scoop into a mixing bowl, then set aside to cool.

Lay the mackerel fillets on a board and run your finger down the centre, working from the head to the tail, feeling for pin bones. If you feel any, nip them out with fish tweezers, then skin the fish as best you can (page 20). Mackerel have thin skin that can be tricky to neatly remove in one go, and to be honest it won't matter at all if it's not the neatest job. Roughly chop the fillets, then drop into a food processor and pulse to a rough purée; some texture is fine. You can also finely chop by hand if you prefer.

Scoop into the bowl with the leek and potato mix and add the horseradish, either fresh grated or sauce. Stir well to mix.

Makes 12–16 rolls

330g (11oz) pack of ready-rolled puff pastry
50g (2oz) butter
2 tbsp olive oil
2 leeks, chopped
300g (10½oz) potatoes, peeled and chopped into 1cm (½in) cubes
a few sprigs of thyme, leaves picked
4 mackerel fillets, pin boned
125g (4oz) fresh horseradish root, grated (or 3 generous tbsp horseradish sauce)
a little flour, for dusting
1 egg, beaten with a pinch of flaked sea salt
1 tbsp black onion seeds
vegetable oil, for greasing
flaked sea salt and freshly ground black pepper

Unroll the pastry onto a lightly floured worktop. Take a rolling pin and roll it just a smidge thinner, then slice down the long side to give you two slim rectangles. Spoon the filling in a line down the centre of each and use your hands to shape into a long sausage. Brush a little beaten egg down one side, then roll the other side up and over to meet it, pressing down firmly to seal. With the joined edge face down, brush more egg all over the top. Sprinkle on the black onion seeds and then use scissors to snip little cuts through the pastry all down the length. Use a sharp knife to cut into individual rolls; you should get around 12–16 depending on the size you want them.

Drizzle just a little vegetable oil onto a baking pan and rub all over. Line up the rolls, taking care that they don't sit too close to the edges where they might sit over the direct heat. At this point you can loosely cover and chill the rolls in the fridge for up to 24 hours, or you can freeze until you want to cook them. Well wrapped, they will store happily for 3 months.

When you are ready to eat them, fire up the barbecue ready for 'baking', with a fire either side and a generous fire-free zone in between, aiming for a lid temperature of 180–200°C (350–400°F). Select a baking tray that will sit on the grill bars between the two fires so you can line up the rolls so none will sit over direct heat. Drizzle just a little vegetable oil onto it and rub all over Line up the rolls, taking care that they don't sit too close to the edges where they might sit over the direct heat.

Set the tray onto the grill bars between the two fires and bake for around 40–45 minutes with the lid down. Check around halfway and rotate the baking tray if necessary.

While the rolls are baking, make the relish on the hob. Simply put everything into a small pan and simmer for a few minutes until the tomatoes have collapsed. Season to taste with salt and pepper. Scoop into a bowl ready to serve alongside the fishage rolls when they come off the barbecue.

For the tomato relish

2 tbsp olive oil
300g (10½oz) cherry tomatoes, halved
3 garlic cloves, sliced
a pinch of sugar, to taste
a shake of chilli sauce (optional)

Chapter 6:
Suckers and shells

This varied and tasty chapter is full of all the things we eat from the sea that aren't fish. So here you find recipes for *cephalopods* (cuttlefish, squid, octopus), *bivalves* (mussels, scallops, clams, oysters) and *crustaceans* (prawns/shrimp, crab, lobster, langoustine). Diverse they may be but if they have one thing in common it's a natural affinity with flavoured butters and oils – they take to richness incredibly well – so once again I urge you to see my recipes as simply ideas to mix and match. Mussels, for example, would be amazing with the whisky seaweed cream I use in the clams recipe (page 230) and prawns would be equally great tossed in the tarragon and chive butter rather than the more spendy langoustine on page 236. Cuttles and squid are interchangeable in cooking and eating terms, although you can't stuff a cuttle because removing the bone splits the body open. Basically what I'm saying is, the world is indeed your oyster …

THE GOOD AND THE BAD

What is 'good' eating in terms of sustainability is at the heart of this book, and the picture is constantly changing, but what I can tell you is that here you get two extremes. With mussels I'm not sure if there is a better, more sustainable protein on the planet. If we want to consume animal proteins, we should all be eating more mussels. Conversely, with lobsters, it's not necessarily that they are 'bad' to eat, but a lobster cannot breed until it's about seven years old (and they can live way, way longer, an unbelievable 72 years is the UK record), so they should be saved for a very rare treat (which should also please your bank account). In loose general terms, the quicker something grows to adulthood, the more likely it is to be sustainable as it will get the chance to reproduce and keep the population of that species growing. When we take more than a species can breed is where the big problems lie. See page 266 for more information on resources and sustainability. Now read on.

Squid and cuttlefish: the cephalopods

In this book I have favoured squid and cuttlefish over octopus. Much as I love it, the current reality is octopus isn't a wise choice, with a long history of overfishing and limited science available on numbers in the seas. Situations change, so do check the resources on page 266 to access the latest status. Both cuttlefish and squid make for excellent eating, and as short-lived, fast-growing species they can be a better choice. However, stocks fluctuate and abundance can often be localized so I still view eating both as a rare treat rather than something I would cook every day or even every month.

How to prepare squid and cuttlefish

Both are best prepped in and near your kitchen sink as it's a messy business. Cuttles are famed for their black ink that can, and no doubt will, get everywhere. Wear an apron, not your best white tee shirt. Obviously this prepping job is something your fishmonger can do as well if you'd rather. Both freeze brilliantly raw for up to 3 months and the freezing process actually helps to tenderize the flesh, so you can feel good about buying when abundant and storing for a later date.

Preparing squid

Under cold running water, twist to pull off the head and tentacles, which may pull out most of the guts too. Take a sharp knife and cut just in front of the eyes to remove the head from the tentacles. Squeeze the tentacles around the mouth to remove the hard beak. Drop the tentacles into a colander and discard the head and beak. Put your fingers inside the body cavity and pull out the thin, clear quill and any remaining guts and discard. Pull away the mottled membrane covering the outside of the body and discard. This outer skin is edible but can go a bit tough on cooking. Trim off the wings from the body – they should pull away fairly easily with your hands. Drop the body and wings into the colander with the tentacles and give everything a really good rinse under cold running water. Drain well and pat dry with paper towel.

Preparing cuttlefish

Under cold running water, twist off the head and tentacles. Make a cut just in front of the eyes to separate the tentacles, discarding the head. Squeeze the tentacles around the mouth to pop out the beak and drop the tentacles into a colander. Then, holding the body firmly in one hand, locate the cuttle bone on the back with the other hand. Grab both sides of the cuttle bone between thumb and fingers and twist it out of the skin and discard (or save it for your pet birds to peck at – my chickens are big fans!). You can then pull apart the body, opening it out like a book by running your thumbs down the softer part under where the cuttle was. Pull off the wings and then work the skin free from the wings and the body using your fingers. Discard the skin and drop the wings and body in the colander. Give everything a good wash under cold running water and then pat dry with paper towel.

Squid with squid-ink aioli and skin-on fries

An easy, treaty supper for two, the fries get cooked on a grill tray, where they get crispy using a high indirect heat (convection currents are amazingly efficient). This tray is one of my favourite bits of barbecue kit, I use it all the time for everything and would urge you to invest in one as I'm sure you'll love it too. By the way, if you really don't fancy the squid ink in the aioli or you can't get hold of any from the fishmongers, just omit it and proceed as per the recipe; it will taste great but just not be as crazily black. Or looked at the opposite way, you could also take some good store-bought mayo and mix in a little ink too.

Drop the cleaned squid tentacles into a mixing bowl. Insert a sharp knife into the bodies and slice open down one side, folding out like a book, then cut each in half down the centre. Score through the inside surface in diagonal criss-cross lines 1cm (½in) or so apart, taking care not to cut all the way through. Add to the bowl, pour over the olive oil and add the garlic, thyme leaves, lemon zest and juice and season with salt and pepper, stirring to mix. Set aside in the fridge for 30–60 minutes.

Scrub the potatoes clean and cut into fries of about 1.5cm (⅝in) thick, tossing into a bowl as you go. Drizzle over the olive oil and sprinkle on the paprika. Add the thyme sprigs, season with salt and pepper and toss to mix.

Fire up barbecue with two small fires down either side and set a grill tray on the grill bars between them. Open the air vents up to give you a temperature of around 200°C (400°F) – see pages 28–31 for fire tips and set-ups.

Tip the potato pieces into the grill tray, spreading them out in an even single layer. Shut the lid and cook indirectly between the fires for about 25–30 minutes, turning over a few times, until golden and crisp.

Serves 2

600–700g (1lb 5oz–1lb 9oz) squid, cleaned and prepped (page 199)
1 tbsp olive oil
1 garlic clove, finely chopped
a few sprigs of thyme, leaves picked
zest of 1 lemon, juice of ½ (use the rest of the juice below)
flaked sea salt and freshly ground black pepper

For the fries

600g (1lb 5oz) potatoes, scrubbed but unpeeled
2 tbsp olive oil
1 tsp hot smoked paprika
a few sprigs of thyme

While the fries are cooking, make the aioli. Due to the smallish quantity, a pestle and mortar and bit of elbow grease is the best way to do this; there is not really enough volume for a blender to be efficient. Add the garlic cloves to the mortar and sprinkle in the salt. Pound with the pestle to crush, then grind around and around to get a creamy paste. Add the egg yolk and squid ink and mix really well with the pestle for a couple of minutes. Then add the oil drop by drop at first, grinding and mixing well between each addition. Once the sauce begins to thicken and emulsify, you can add the oil a little quicker but take care not to overdo the flow as the aioli might split. Once all the oil is in, you should be left with a dark and creamy sauce. Add the lemon juice and stir well before spooning into a serving bowl. You can also make in a bowl with a whisk, crushing the garlic first, then following the same method.

Once the fries are cooked, scoop into a bowl and take them inside to keep warm. Make sure your coals are really hot, so get the lid up for maximum oxygen, and add a little more fuel if necessary. Set the grill tray back over the fire and grill the squid over a searingly high heat for just a couple of minutes, turning a few times. Start with the tentacles first, as they take a little longer, then add the rest cut-side down first.

To serve, scatter the leaves over a platter, pile on the fries and nestle the bowl of aioli on one side. Top with the squid and perhaps a little extra sprinkle of salt, plus more lemon for squeezing over as you eat.

For the aioli
2 fat garlic cloves
1 tsp flaked sea salt
1 egg yolk
1 tsp squid ink (or cuttle ink)
100ml (3½fl oz/scant ½ cup) rapeseed oil
juice of ½ a lemon (from above)

To serve
1 soft head of lettuce, leaves separated,
    washed and dried
lemon, for squeezing (optional)

Stuffed hasselback squid with orzo, 'nduja and basil

Here squid gets the 'hasselback' treatment where the body has a series of slits cut into it on both sides, giving a concertina effect if you gently pull at each end. More than just an Instagram-worthy technique, the slits increase the surface area and allow the oils from the stuffing to seep out when cooking, giving you more delicious crispy bits. If I can find one, I like to make this with a single big squid that I carve at the table like a generous fat sausage. You can use smaller squid (or even lots of baby ones) but it will mean cooking time is a bit quicker, and my stuffing quantities may give you a little more or less than you need.

A note on the ingredients here. Orzo are little rice-shaped 'grains' of pasta that make a lovely, sticky filling. If you can't get any, then any mini pasta would work, or even cooked rice would be fine. 'Nduja is a powerhouse of an ingredient, a spreadably soft salami that adds both chilli heat and deep savoury flavour. Sadly, it's not the easiest ingredient to source so if you can't find it, add a little finely chopped cooking chorizo pimped up with a pinch of chilli powder to taste. As always, the internet is your friend for anything you can't get locally.

For the stuffing, cook the pasta in plenty of lightly salted boiling water until just al dente, then drain and run under cold water to stop any further cooking. Tip into a mixing bowl and toss through a drizzle of oil to stop the grains sticking together.

Set a heavy-based saucepan over a low heat on the hob and pour in the olive oil. Add the onion and allow it to cook gently for a good 20–30 minutes until it is really soft and lightly caramelized. Add the garlic, season with salt and pepper and stir for a minute or so, then add the 'nduja. Allow it to melt into the onions, then turn up the heat and let it cook for a few minutes until you have a gloriously brick-red mass. Pour in the wine and allow it to reduce and evaporate, stirring every now and then so it doesn't burn on the base. Turn off the heat and stir through the basil, then pour into the bowl of cooled pasta. Set aside to go cold while you prep the squid.

Score one side of the squid wings very lightly in a criss-cross pattern with a sharp knife and leave the tentacles whole. Insert a wooden rolling pin gently into the squid body all the way to the end. Take a super-sharp knife and cut slices about 5mm (¼in) apart through the flesh down to the rolling pin. Rotate the pin

Serves 2–4, depending on what else you are eating

1 large squid (about 750g (1lb 10oz) or a couple of smaller ones, cleaned and prepped (page 199)

For the stuffing

200g (7oz) orzo pasta
3 tbsp olive oil, plus extra for drizzling
1 large red onion, finely chopped
1 garlic, crushed to a paste
80g (3oz) 'nduja
100ml (3½fl oz/scant ½ cup) white wine
50g (2oz) basil, chopped, minus fattest stalks
flaked sea salt and freshly ground black pepper

and the squid with it, and cut again on the other side. If you are using smaller squid, think about using the handle of a wooden spoon or spatula; you want to be able to support the body so you cut thin slices without penetrating all the way through and out the other side.

Spoon the cold filling into the body, pushing it down firmly so the whole body is full; it should be quite round and firm. Use a few cocktail sticks (toothpicks) to close and secure the open end as best you can, but don't stress to seal it completely as it should hold together. Drizzle a little olive oil all over the outside and over the tentacles and wings and sprinkle generously with salt. You can prep and stuff the squid and chill it in the fridge for up to 24 hours if you want to get ahead.

Fire up the barbecue with the coals piled to one half so you have a fire-free side to move the squid to finish cooking. Let the coals get really hot and rest a grill tray over them to heat up.

Once the fire is ready (see page 31), rest the stuffed squid onto the hot grill tray. Cook over a hot heat, turning regularly so all sides become golden brown and crispy. Slide the tray off the fire to the other side of the barbecue and shut the lid, leaving it to finish cooking gently until the filling is piping hot – a temperature probe should read 70°C (158°F) or more in the centre. Open the lid and grill the tentacles and wings over a really hot fire for just a couple of minutes – adding a couple of little fist-sized pieces of smoking wood (page 139) to the hot coals will create some pretty instant hot flames and a nice little smoky hit.

Remove the squid to a board and carve into slices, scatter with the crispy tentacles and wings. Squeeze over plenty of fresh lemon juice and a really generous drizzle of extra virgin olive oil, adding a little extra grind of salt and pepper and a sprinkling of basil, if you like.

To serve
1 lemon, cut into wedges
extra virgin olive oil
a little extra basil, roughly
   chopped

Cuttle and samphire with whipped squash and mint dressing

Pretty as a picture, this tapas-style cuttle dish is full of textures, colours and flavours – these things make eating a joy to me. To create layers of flavour you do need to prep different elements, but you can get the squash ready well ahead of time (even a few days is fine), marinate the cuttles and make the dressing an hour before, then it's just a very quick flash over a very high heat and you're done. A grill tray is once again supremely useful here, allowing you to essentially stir-fry both cuttles and samphire over the fire.

Set a large pan of water over a high heat on the hob, add a pinch of salt and bring to the boil. Drop in the squash and simmer for about 5–8 minutes until tender. Drain and leave to steam dry in the colander for a few minutes before dropping into a food processor or food mixer fitted with a paddle beater.

Add the garlic, cumin and a good seasoning of salt and pepper and whizz or beat until smooth. Spoon in the yogurt and mix to blend, then, with the motor running, drizzle in the oil until you have a smooth creamy paste. Spoon into a bowl and set aside. It will keep for up to 3 days in the fridge but is best served at room temperature, so get it out well before serving.

An hour before you want to cook, cut the cuttle bodies into 5mm (¼in) strips, slice the wings into similar-sized strips and cut the tentacles into individual strands. Drop the lot into a mixing bowl and add the samphire, olive oil, garlic and cumin. Season well with salt and pepper and stir to mix. Slide into the fridge to marinate for an hour or so.

In a small bowl, whisk together the olive oil for the dressing with the lemon juice, honey and mint. Season to taste with salt and pepper and store in the fridge until you are ready to serve.

Fire up your barbecue ready for hot direct grilling (page 31). You won't need much fuel, as the cuttle and samphire both cook super-fast. Leave the lid off your barbecue to allow the charcoal to burn with maximum oxygen and set a grill tray over the fire to heat up.

Spread the whipped squash over a plate or two – I like to make a couple of plates to serve one at either end of the table – using the back of the spoon to create a few dips and furrows.

Serves 4

750g (1lb 10oz) cuttles, cleaned and prepped (page 199)
150g (5oz) samphire
3 tbsp olive oil
3 garlic cloves, crushed to a paste
1 heaped tbsp cumin seeds, toasted and crushed

For the squash

500g (1lb 2oz) squash, peeled, deseeded and chopped into 3–4cm (1¼–1½in) chunks
2 garlic cloves
2 tbsp cumin seeds, toasted and ground
3 tbsp Greek yogurt
75ml (5 tbsp) extra virgin olive oil
flaked sea salt and freshly ground black pepper

For the mint dressing

50ml extra virgin olive oil
juice of ½–1 lemon, to taste
1 tbsp runny honey
15g (½oz) mint, leaves picked

Tip the cuttle and samphire onto the hot grill tray and stir-fry over a very high heat for just a couple of minutes until lightly charred. Then tip on top of the squash and drizzle over the dressing. Sprinkle over the pecans, then scatter with the extra mint, and pul biber or chilli flakes if you like, and serve straight away with flatbreads or sourdough toast.

To garnish

50g (2oz/½ cup) pecans, toasted and roughly chopped

a few mint leaves, roughly chopped

1–2 tsp pul biber, or a pinch of dried chilli (hot pepper) flakes (optional)

flatbreads, or sourdough toast, to serve

Cuttlefish satay with sambal kecap and grilled pak choi

Cuttles get the Indonesian satay treatment, marinated in soy and spices and cooked very hot and fast so they stay tender. Squid would work equally well but at certain times cuttlefish are abundant along the south coast of the UK so make a good sustainable and economical option. Kecap manis is a sweet soy sauce that's fairly easy to find but use regular soy and add a couple of teaspoons of brown sugar if you struggle.

Take a mixing bowl and pour in the oyster sauce, kecap manis and sesame oil. Stir through the ginger, garlic and peppercorns until well mixed. Drop the cuttle tentacles into the marinade. Then slice the bodies into 1cm (½in) strips, dropping into the marinade as you go. Stir really well, then slide into the fridge to marinate for an hour.

Fire up the barbecue ready for hot direct grilling (page 31). Make sure that the fire is good and hot, so leave the lid off and the vents open for maximum oxygen flow.

To make the sambal, stir together the kecap manis, lime juice and zest, chilli, garlic and shallot. Pour into a little serving dish.

Prepare the pak choi for grilling by slicing it into wedges through the base, cutting each head into 4–6 wedges. Spread out on a baking sheet and drizzle over a little sesame oil.

Thread the cuttlefish onto skewers, ribboning each strip on the stick so it's secure; reserve any extra marinade to baste. Line up on a tray or plate and take to the barbecue along with the remaining marinade and the pak choi.

Rest the pak choi on the grill bars over the fire and cook for a couple of minutes on each side until lightly charred with a little crunch left. Slide off the heat away from the fire to keep warm.

Lay the skewers on the grill bars over the hot fire and cook over high heat for just 2–3 minutes, basting with the extra marinade and turning once or twice until they are lightly charred.

To serve, pile the pak choi onto a platter, nestle the bowl of sambal to one side and top with the skewers. Best eaten hot straight from the grill.

Serves 4

3 tbsp oyster sauce
3 tbsp kecap manis (sweet soy sauce)
2 tbsp sesame oil, plus extra to drizzle
50g (2oz) ginger root, grated
4 garlic cloves, chopped
1 tbsp black peppercorns, crushed
1kg (2lb 4oz) cuttlefish, cleaned and prepped (page 199)
400g (14oz) pak choi (bok choy)

For the sambal

5 tbsp kecap manis (sweet soy sauce)
zest and juice of 2 limes
3–4 bird's-eye chillies, finely sliced, to taste
2 garlic cloves, very finely chopped
1 banana shallot, very finely chopped

You also need 8 small or 4 large metal skewers

Mussels, scallops, oysters, clams: the bivalves

Bivalves, literally meaning 'two halves', are all the shellfish with double hinged shells – and here are my recipes for mussels, scallops, oysters and clams.

THREE MUSSEL RECIPES

Mussels – a truly positive seafood choice

Mussels are probably the most sustainable seafood you can put on your table and we should all be eating more of them. Farmed mussels, which are by far the easiest and best to buy, have a very low impact on the environment – they filter out all the food they need from the seawater that flows around them, meaning they require zero extra food to grow to maturity, they need no chemical fertilizers or antibiotic interventions and the greenhouse gas emissions are negligible. On top of that, they are brilliant at cleaning the water around them, and the mussel beds with their long dangling ropes make brilliant wildlife havens for other marine life to shelter around, increasing biodiversity. The fact that they are delicious, cheap and extremely nutritious is a bonus.

How to cook bivalves over fire

In all the recipes that follow you will see I suggest using a grill tray, one of my favourite bits of barbecue kit (page 24) – a thin metal perforated tray that is very useful for cooking fish of all kinds, allowing the smoke through to add flavour while ensuring you don't lose anything to the fire. You could, of course, also use a flameproof frying pan to great effect, although the smoke flavour will be a little less prominent.

Mussels with orange, bay and vermouth

I have to say the sauce here is quite a glorious thing, fragrant and a little sweet and just works so well with plump mussels. It's a breeze to make and so flexible – try it with clams, or simply poured over any grilled fish – I hope it becomes very much part of your seafood repertoire! I like to serve these with lots of crusty bread and peppery watercress, both of which are very nice dunked and drenched in the buttery sauce.

Tip the mussels into a colander and wash well under cold running water, pulling off any beard threads and discarding any mussels that do not close when firmly tapped on the side of the sink. Leave to drain in the colander.

Fire up the barbecue ready for direct grilling. You can, and I often do, add a lump of smoking wood (page 139) to lend a smoky flavour, or you could cook over an open wood fire.

While the fire is heating up, set a deep, flameproof frying pan on the grill bars over the fire (only do this if you are using good, pure charcoal with no chemicals – see page 12 – otherwise you need to wait until the charcoal is fully burnt before you cook). Tip the butter into the pan and, as it melts, add the onion, bay leaves and orange zest. Cook over a medium–high heat for around 20 minutes until the onion is softening and lightly caramelized. Slide away from the heat.

Set a grill tray over the fire and tip on the washed mussels. Shut the lid of the barbecue, or cover loosely with foil if you are cooking on an open fire, to trap in the convection heat that will help the mussels steam open. Cook for around 5 minutes, or until they have all opened up. Discard any that refuse to open, then tip the rest into the pan with the buttery onions, pulling it back over the heat to get hot.

Pour the vermouth over the mussels, squeeze in the orange juice and season with salt and pepper. Let it bubble away and reduce for a few minutes before serving.

Serves 2 generously

1kg (2lb 4oz) mussels
75g (2½oz) butter
1 onion, finely chopped
6 bay leaves, finely sliced
1 orange, zest peeled off in thick
   strips, plus juice
200ml (7fl oz/scant 1 cup) white
   vermouth
flaked sea salt and freshly ground
   black pepper

To serve
watercress
crusty bread

Lemongrass and coconut mussels

A big bowl of Thai-style mussels, fragrant with citrussy lemongrass, was one of the first things my husband cooked for me many moons ago. Here's my version, albeit cooked over fire rather than on the hob, although you could, like so many of the recipes here, take this inside your kitchen if you prefer.

I confess I would probably be found eating these with chips (a South East Asian version of chips and curry sauce – why on earth not?!) but rice would work nicely too.

Tip the mussels into a colander and wash thoroughly under cold running water. Pull away and discard any beards, along with any mussels that don't shut when tapped firmly on the side of the sink. Leave to drain in the colander while you light the fire. Just as on the previous page, you can cook this recipe with pure charcoal, or add a little wood for smoke or cook over an open wood fire.

Set a deep frying pan over the fire and pour in the oil. Add the shallots, garlic, lemongrass and chillies and fry gently over a medium heat for about 15 minutes until the shallot is softening, stirring from time to time to make sure it's cooking evenly. Pour in the fish sauce and stir briefly to evaporate, then add the coconut milk and lime leaves and season with a little salt and pepper. Simmer for 10 minutes or so until thickened, then set aside and keep warm.

Set a grill tray over the fire and tip in the cleaned mussels. Shut the lid of the barbecue, or cover loosely with foil if you are cooking on an open fire, and leave to cook for around 5 minutes until they have all opened. Discard any that refuse to open.

Tip the cooked mussels into the pan of sauce, setting back over the fire to heat up a little, if necessary, and toss together to mix. Sprinkle with fresh herbs and serve immediately with your choice of carb.

Serves 2 generously

1kg (2lb 4oz) mussels
2 tbsp vegetable oil
3 large banana shallots, about
    160g (5½oz), finely chopped
4 fat garlic cloves, sliced
2 lemongrass stalks, finely sliced
1–3 bird's-eye chillies, sliced,
    to taste
3 tbsp fish sauce
400ml (13fl oz/generous 1½ cups)
    can of coconut milk
4 double-lobed lime leaves,
    finely sliced
flaked sea salt and freshly ground
    black pepper

To serve

Thai basil or coriander (cilantro),
    roughly chopped
a carb of your choosing

Smoked mussels with panko and thyme crumbs

A slightly different way to do mussels, whereby you briefly steam to open them up before smoking with crispy crumbs on top. Don't stint on the olive oil, its essential for flavour, crunch and unctuousness. This is a perfect bar snack, quick to cook and fun to nibble before you crank up the heat on the grill to cook a main course.

Fire up your barbecue ready for indirect smoking, aiming for a temperature of 140°C (284°F); see pages 28–31 for fire tips.

Tip the cleaned mussels into a saucepan, then cover with a tight-fitting lid and set over a high heat on the hob. Steam briefly for a couple of minutes, just until they open up. Tip onto a tray and allow to cool for a few minutes until you can handle them without burning your fingers.

Weigh the panko into a small bowl and stir through the finely chopped garlic and thyme leaves. Season well with salt and pepper. Set aside.

Pull the mussels open and tear off the top shell, leaving the mussel meat intact in the lower shell. If the meat is a little stuck between two shells, use an empty half shell as a scoop to tease it away. Discard the empty halves and line up all the half shells with the meat in on a grill tray; pushing them snugly together will help keep them upright.

Sprinkle a little of the crumb mixture into each mussel, then generously drizzle in the olive oil so it coats the crumbs and makes a little puddle in the base of each shell.

Take the tray to the barbecue and set onto the grill bars away from the smoky fire. Shut the lid to keep the temperature low and trap the smoke in.

Cook for 15–20 minutes until the tops are lightly golden and crispy. Pull the tray off the grill and tuck in straight away, cold beers at the ready.

Serves 4–6 as a snack, less as a more substantial meal

1kg (2lb 4oz) mussels, cleaned and bearded (page 213)
50g (2oz/1 cup) panko breadcrumbs
2 fat garlic cloves, finely chopped
a few bushy sprigs of thyme, leaves picked and finely chopped
about 4 tbsp extra virgin olive oil
flaked sea salt and freshly ground black pepper

THREE HALF-SHELL SCALLOP RECIPES

Scallops are an absolute delight to cook over the fire and feel like a real treat of a thing to eat. Super-quick to cook and they also rather handily come with their own little grill tray so no extra equipment is necessary.

How green is your scallop?

As ever, the sustainability picture can be a little muddled. Commercially the traditional way has always been dredging the seabed to scoop them up from the sandy bottom where they live. Dredging for our seafood is generally thought to be pretty destructive and therefore a bad thing, but in the case of scallops you could argue the case for it a little more. Scallops live on bare open sand beds where the water often flows pretty fast, meaning the seabed is constantly moving and shifting with wave action. It's not a stable environment and as such it's quite a specialized niche that isn't generally that rich in other marine life. Dredging is not a fine art and invariably scallops will get missed, meaning they live to fight (and breed) another day. As long as one area is not dredged over and over, populations can remain pretty healthy. Hand diving for scallops is generally considered the 'gold standard' by many, but actually a diver may take most of the scallops within a certain area because eyes and hands are way more accurate and efficient than a dredger, so an area where too many divers have taken too many scallops is also bad. There are healthy scallop grounds and scallop grounds that have been over-fished, so it's worth checking the current picture using the resources on page 266. Like mussels, scallops can also be farmed successfully and this is a growing industry that's worth supporting. The Marine Stewardship Council (MSC) give farmed scallops, like farmed mussels, a rating of 1, meaning they are a 'best-choice' species when it comes to eating seafood.

How to prep a whole scallop

Very often the scallops we buy will be sold in the 'half-shell', meaning all the prep work has been done for you. If they come whole, or you have gathered them yourself (which I once did on a scuba trip in Scotland many years ago – still one of the most memorable meals of my life), then here's what to do.

With the scallop the deep rounded shell-side down, use a small, sharp knife and insert the tip between the two shells. Give the knife a little twist and prise the two shells apart. Discard the flat top shell. Use a spoon to scoop out the scallop from the bottom shell and trim off any black and frilly bits; you want to be left just with the white scallop and the pinky-orange coral. Wash the scallop under cold running water, pat dry and line up on a plate. Chill until you are ready to cook – they will be happy for a few hours in the fridge. Wash the deeper bottom shell and dry, reserving to use in the recipes as a little grill tray.

Fizz-flamed scallops, caper, sage and hazelnut butter

Something of a speedy, dare I say it, date-night dish. Decadent but easy. This recipe is an ode to my pal Simon Stallard, all-round good guy and fire-cooking demon, who is famed for his theatrical spraying of champagne over scallops. I am no fizz aficionado and am quite content to stick to cava or Crémant, but whatever you use, make sure it's nicely chilled and perfectly drinkable on its own.

Fire up the barbecue ready for direct grilling. Scallops cook super-fast so you won't need more than a thin layer of hot charcoal or hot wood embers.

Rest the empty scallop shells directly over the fire, or nestle directly in the embers, and leave to get hot for a few minutes. Test how hot they are by flicking a few drops of water onto them; the water should sizzle and evaporate almost instantly.

While the shells are heating, set a small flameproof pan (no plastic or wooden handles) over the fire and tip in the hazelnuts, allowing them to toast for a couple of minutes before adding the butter. As it melts, add the garlic, capers, sage and pul biber. Season well with salt and pepper and stir to mix, then slide the pan off the fire.

When the shells are hot, put the scallops back in and pour the hot butter over the top. Cook for just a few minutes until the butter is bubbling and the scallops are opaque. Pour the fizz quickly over the scallops – you can pour freestyle from the bottle, or you may find it easier to use a jug – and let it bubble furiously for another minute.

Use tongs to transfer the shells carefully to a warmed plate, taking care not to let any of the precious sauce spill out. Tuck in while hot, with plenty of crusty bread to mop up the sauce. And, obviously, the rest of the bottle of fizz alongside.

Serves 2

6 large, fat, half-shell scallops, cleaned and prepped (see opposite)

75g (2½oz) hazelnuts, roughly chopped

75g (2½oz) butter

3 garlic cloves, thinly sliced

2 tbsp little pickled capers, drained

a loose handful of sage leaves, about 12, roughly chopped

2 tsp pul biber flakes

about 200ml (7fl oz/scant 1 cup) fizz or white wine

flaked sea salt and freshly ground black pepper

Scallops with orange, basil and caper dressing

A simple grilled scallop with a fresh, zesty dressing, I think these make a lovely decadent bar snack to eat before you get on and cook the main event. To make it super-speedy you can get the dressing ready a few hours ahead, but don't add the basil until you are ready to serve, as it will discolour and loose its vibrancy.

Begin with the dressing. Mix the olive oil, orange zest and juice, garlic and capers in a small bowl. Season to taste with salt and pepper. If you are cooking immediately, stir through the basil. If not, chill the dressing the fridge and add the basil just before cooking the scallops.

Fire up the barbecue ready for direct grilling. Scallops grill fast so you won't need too much fuel, depending on what else you are going on to cook.

Rest the empty scallop shells on the grill bars over the fire, or nestle directly in the embers, and leave to get hot for a few minutes. Test how hot they are by flicking a few drops of water onto them; the water should sizzle and evaporate almost instantly.

When the shells are hot, drizzle just a little olive oil over the scallops and season with salt and pepper, tossing gently to coat. Quickly drop a scallop into each hot shell and let it sear for a minute or so until lightly golden. Use small tongs or a fork to turn each scallop over and cook for another minute or so on the other side.

Once cooked, spread out over a platter and spoon a little dressing over the top. Serve immediately.

Serves 4–6 as a snack
12 half-shell scallops, cleaned and prepped (page 220)
olive oil, to drizzle

For the dressing
100ml (3½fl oz/scant ½ cup) extra virgin olive oil
zest and juice of 1 large orange
2 garlic cloves, crushed to a paste
50g (2oz) capers, drained
a good handful of basil leaves, about 30g (1oz)
flaked sea salt and freshly ground black pepper

Scallops and cannellini beans with burnt bay and porcini oil

A slightly more hearty and wholesome scallop dish than the previous two. Yes, butter can be wholesome, especially if you throw some beans in the mix. Again this is super-quick, bar the mushroom soaking time, so you won't need a great deal of fuel for cooking, but the heat will need to be under all the scallops, so spread your embers out onto a thin, even layer. You can cook in a couple of batches if necessary.

Put the porcini in a heatproof glass or mug, pour over boiling water to cover and set aside to soak for 30 minutes. Fish out with a fork, roughly chop and add to a small heatproof frying pan along with the olive oil and garlic. Strain the liquid through a sieve and reserve.

Use a small knife to ease the scallops from their shells and set aside on a plate ready to take to the barbecue, along with the empty shells and the pan with the porcini and garlic.

Fire up the barbecue ready for direct hot grilling, spreading the coals in a thin, even layer so each scallop will be over direct heat. Once the fire is hot, set the lemon halves, cut-side down on the grill bars to lightly char them. Rest the bay leaves on the grill bars and lightly burn them – this will take mere seconds so do stay with them. Remove the bay leaves to a board and finely chop before adding to the pan with the porcini and garlic.

Set the pan over the fire and fry for a couple of minutes to soften the garlic. Tip in the beans and add the reserved porcini soaking liquid. Season well with salt and pepper, then leave to sizzle over a high heat for a couple of minutes. Slide the pan away from the heat.

Rest the empty scallop shells over the fire, popping a cube of butter into each. Depending on the amount of grill space you have, you may need to cook them in two batches but they cook so quickly you won't keep anyone waiting too long to eat.

Once the butter is sizzling, put a scallop back into each shell, cooking for a minute or so before turning over. Once the scallops are all turned, spoon the beans and porcini on top. Finish with a squeeze of the charred lemon juice and serve immediately.

Serves 4

10g (⅓oz) dried porcini
6 tbsp olive oil
3 garlic cloves, thinly sliced
12 large half-shell scallops, cleaned and prepped (page 220)
1 lemon, halved
6 large fresh bay leaves
400g (14oz) can of cannellini beans, drained and rinsed
60g (2oz) butter, cut into 12 little cubes
flaked sea salt and freshly ground black pepper

Grilled oysters with kimchi butter

I like to cook these oysters very briefly over a bed of extremely hot embers, nestling the shells directly on the coals to keep them upright so you don't lose precious liquor or butter. The kimchi butter is ridiculously easy but packed full of flavour. The hardest part of this dish is getting the oysters shucked, which is a bit of a fiddle but you could always ask your fishmonger to do it for you. These take a minute or even less to cook, so consider them a decadent little nibble before you go on to cook something else over the fire.

Begin by opening, or 'shucking', the oysters. A stiff and blunt shucking knife is the best tool for the job. Grab a clean tea towel and fold over and over to give you a thick pad to protect your hand. If you are right handed, lay the folded towel across your left palm and sit an oyster, rounded-side down on top with the hinge facing your right hand. Fold the towel over the top to protect your hand, then insert the tip of the shucking knife into the hinge that joins the top and bottom shell. It may take a bit of force to get it in, hence the towel for grip and protection. Once the tip is in twist the knife firmly to prise the shells apart. Then slide the knife across the underside of the top shell to release the oyster. Discard the top shell and then use the knife to release the oyster from where it is connected to the bottom shell. Set on a tray, balancing against the edge of the tray if necessary to make sure the oyster stays upright. Repeat. Slide into the fridge while you get the fire hot.

Light the barbecue ready for hot direct cooking, spreading the coals out into a thin, even layer – they need to take up the same amount of space as the oysters on the tray. Leave the lid off the barbecue to get the fire burning really hot, and remove the grill bars so you can cook directly on the embers. This is a great thing to cook on a hot open fire too.

Set a small flameproof pan on the embers and drop in the butter and kimchi, then season with salt and pepper and allow to melt and bubble for a minute or so. Slide the pan off the coals to one side so it stays hot.

Using a gloved hand, and working as quickly as you can, nestle the oysters on top of the hot coals. Spoon the hot butter over and allow it to bubble furiously for just a minute or so. Remove to a plate, sprinkle over the spring onions and eat straight away.

Serves 4–6 as a snack

12 large oysters
100g (3½oz) butter
50g (2oz) kimchi, finely chopped
3 spring onions (scallions),
    finely sliced
flaked sea salt and freshly ground
    black pepper

Clams with whisky seaweed cream

Clams are another wonderfully sweet bivalve, and they go so well with a good splash of whisky in this creamy sauce. Mussels would work brilliantly too, or indeed make the sauce to pour over any grilled fish. Seek out dried seaweed online – it's becoming a much more commonplace ingredient, packed full of nutrients and full of flavour. Here I used sea spaghetti from the Cornish Seaweed Co. (page 266). I like to eat these piled on top of spaghetti, but crusty bread would be great too.

Put the dried seaweed in a bowl and cover with boiling water. Set aside for 15 minutes until soft, then drain and finely chop.

Tip the clams into a colander and wash well under cold running water. Discard any that don't slowly close when you tap them gently against the side of the sink. Tip into a bowl ready to take to the barbecue.

Light a barbecue or open fire ready for hot direct grilling but leaving a space with no fire so you have some heat control (page 31). Add a couple of lumps of smoking wood to the fire for smoky clams.

Set a deep, flameproof frying pan over the fire as it heats and drop in the butter to melt. Add the chopped seaweed and the red onion and fry gently for 15–20 minutes until lightly caramelized and soft. Control the heat by sliding the pan slightly off the fire.

Stir through the garlic for a minute or so, then pour the whisky into the pan and allow it to bubble and reduce for a couple of minutes over a high heat. Add the cream and season well with salt and pepper, stirring until bubbling hot. Slide the pan off the heat and keep it warm.

Set a grill tray over the fire and tip on the clams. Shut the lid of the barbecue, or cover the tray loosely with foil if you are cooking on an open fire. This will just help steam the clams open. Check after 5 minutes or so, using tongs to toss the clams around so they cook evenly.

Once they are all open, drop the clams into the pan of sauce and stir through. Sprinkle with the chives and serve with your choice of carbs.

Serves 2

15g (½oz) dried seaweed
1kg (2lb 4oz) clams
50g (2oz) butter
1 red onion, finely chopped
3 garlic cloves, finely chopped
3 tbsp whisky
100ml (3½fl oz/scant ½ cup) double (heavy) cream
flaked sea salt and freshly ground black pepper
a handful of snipped chives, to garnish

To serve
your choice of carbs

Crabs, lobsters, prawns and langoustine: the crustaceans

Some of the best, and most luxurious, things you can bung over your fire. Here are a few recipes for crabs, lobsters, prawns and langoustines, collectively known as the crustaceans. They have one major thing in common: a hard external skeleton, the shell, and no internal bones. The flavour of the meat is mild and sweet and is pretty much always enhanced by some sort of rich butter-based sauce. The other thing to note is that there's tonnes of flavour in the actual shells themselves, so it's always a good thing to scoop them up after eating to make stock (page 35).

Crab and lobster

I do prefer the flavour of crab meat to lobster but there is no denying they are more fiddly to eat. With lobster you get a good chunk of body meat that's brilliant grilled and doused in – guess what? – something buttery. With crab, the bulk of the good eating, especially with the spider crabs, comes from the legs. There is no body meat as such. So what I tend to do is chop them up into leg sections before grilling from raw, saving the body shell for stock (page 35) and the brown meat for bisque (page 37) or pasta. Then, once cooked, you just need to roll up your sleeves and get stuck in, with plenty of napkins and warm lemony water on hand for washing sticky paws as you go.

How to dispatch a live one
A rare occurrence saved for an occasional treat, if I am buying crab or lobster I would also always favour buying online directly from a specialist crustacean merchant (page 266) and much prefer to buy them live and cook them fresh – the flavour and texture cannot be beaten. But it does mean you need to dispatch and cook them as quickly as you can after purchase. As a warning, prepping a raw crustacean is a messy and perhaps somewhat gruesome job not to be tackled if you are squeamish about these things. You can also make the recipes that follow using ready-cooked crab or lobster, in which case you are just reheating them on the fire.

Killing an animal is never an easy thing but by putting a live lobster or crab in the freezer for a couple of hours you will send it into a dormant state, a hibernation of sorts, which is considered the most humane approach as it renders the animal insensible. Then you will need to mechanically and speedily kill it through its nerve centres before you cook it. Plunging live animals into boiling water is definitely no longer considered an acceptable way to kill them. You will need a good, big freezer for quick and efficient chilling; an ice compartment above your fridge that's rammed full of half eaten tubs of ice cream just isn't going to cut it.

And, then once rendered insensible …

With a lobster

Lobster have a good meaty body that grills really well from raw, so my preference is to kill with a sharp knife, then cut in half down the length of the body. Take the lobster from the freezer and rest it legs down on a board. Locate the clearly defined cross on the back of shell, a few centimetres behind the eyes, and pierce the tip of the knife quickly down through the head. This will instantly kill the already dormant animal. Then you can slice all the way down through the body and tail to give you two halves. Remove and discard the stomach sac and dark intestine thread.

With a crab (brown or spider)

With crab, the bulk of the meat – especially in spider crabs – is in the legs rather than in the body, so you don't get a neat body to grill. To kill a crab, remove from the freezer and rest belly-side up on a board. Crabs have two nerve centres that need 'spiking' to kill. Raise the tail flap and you will see a small hole underneath. Take a heavy sharp knife and a mallet and give the top of the knife handle a sharp tap to insert the blade quickly down through the hole to the shell on the other side. The other nerve centre is a small depression towards the head end of the underside. Insert the knife quickly here too, again using a mallet to tap it firmly in. The animal is now dead.

Brown crab or spider crab?

I love both but spider crabs are particularly sustainable and abundant. Popular on the European continent, which is where most of the spider crabs are exported to, it would be great to see them get a popularity boost in the UK as the meat is very tasty indeed. They do suffer a little from an image problem, which may be why a recent rebranding effort calls them Cornish King crab. As a bit of an arachnophobe, I do wonder if the name is partly responsible as well as the gangly leggy appearance. In the recipe overleaf I used brown crabs, and I used the spiders for Sri Lankan crab curry (page 253), but both recipes are interchangeable. The other good thing about spiders? Half the price of brown crab.

How to eat crab legs

Given that a whole crab is a rare treat for most of us, a little guidance on the method of attack when eating is probably useful. You can buy a 'crab claw cracker', a bit like a nut cracker, but I find they are a bit too much for the job, prone to leaving tiny bits of shell because of over exertion of pressure. I use a more gentle approach, so a rolling pin or other blunt instrument like a mallet. Just tap, tap, tap to crack the shell in a few different places, before using your fingers to peel off the shells. Remember to save all the shells for stock – they really are tasty so this is 100% worth doing (page 35). Then you will need something to help winkle out the meat from the crevices and I find one of the crab's own pincers to be a perfect tool. Anything quite small and pointy would work: a cocktail stick (toothpick), a kebab skewer, maybe even a very slim pickle fork if you happen to have one.

Grilled crab legs with Scotch bonnet and thyme butter

Whether you are using a spider or a brown crab, this recipe takes the raw crab claws and legs and grills them, no pre-boiling required. The main body does not have a whole lot of grill-able meat in it, but plenty of very tasty brown meat, so I would reserve it for making stock, using the brown meat to make the bisque (page 37) or for stirring into pasta dishes. I adore Scotch bonnet chillies for their fruity flavour and fiery heat, but use a milder chilli if you like.

Once you have dispatched the crabs, you can remove the legs from the body. They should twist off fairly easily and may stay joined as a cluster of legs and a claw from each side, or they may separate into individual legs – either is fine. There is plenty of meat around the attachment point of legs to body, so make sure you keep that 'knuckle' on. Remove the gills and guts from the carapace (the body shell) and discard. Scoop out the brown meat and reserve for a bisque (page 37) – you can freeze it – and save the shell for making stock (page 35) – you can freeze that too!

Rest the legs on a chopping board and take a sturdy blunt instrument – a rolling pin or mallet is ideal – and use it to bash and crack open each leg and claw in a few places. You are not looking to remove any meat from the shell but just to split the shell in a few places so the heat, smoke and butter can penetrate.

Fire up the barbecue or a fire pit ready for hot direct grilling, spreading out the hot coals to a thin, even layer that takes up as much space as the crab legs.

Drop the butter into a flameproof pan and set over the grill bars to melt. Add the garlic, thyme leaves, chilli and sugar, season well with salt and pepper and stir over a gentle heat for a few minutes. Pour half into a small serving bowl and set aside, then slide the pan slightly off the heat.

Spread the cracked legs and claws on the grill bars over the fire. Turn and baste with the rest of the butter over a high heat for about 5–6 minutes. Transfer to a large platter or board and tuck in the dish of reserved butter for dipping into as you eat. Serve the lot with plenty of crusty bread and tuck in. For some advice on the best way to get to the crab meat, turn back to page 233.

Serves 2–4 depending on what else you are eating
2 live brown or spider crabs, about 1.5–1.8kg (3lb 5oz–3lb 14oz) each

For the butter
250g (9oz) butter, softened
3 garlic cloves, crushed
a loose handful of thyme sprigs
1–2 Scotch bonnet chillies, cut into quarters
2 tsp soft brown sugar
flaked sea salt and freshly ground black pepper

To serve
crusty bread

Grilled lobster, Pernod beurre blanc

My local fishmonger, 'Sam the Fish' of Bristol Fish, suggested this sauce to me as we were chatting shellfish over the ice counter. Pernod has such a strong smell when you open the bottle, you might feel it would be overwhelming, but by the time it is cooked it just gives a very subtle aniseedy tang in this buttery sauce. If you hate Pernod, just swap it for white wine. The trick to beurre blanc is keeping the butter cold and whisking in a piece at a time over a low heat. If the butter is too soft, or the heat too high, you risk it splitting. Have a few ice cubes on hand and if it looks to be separating, drop one in off the heat and whisk like fury.

You could, of course, serve your grilled lobster with any of the butters, or mayonnaises, in this book and you would have yourself a delicious treat.

Firstly freeze and mechanically kill and split the lobster into half lengthways (page 233). Take a heavy blunt instrument and crack open the claws in a few places, as described in the crab recipe on the previous page. Drizzle the flesh side with olive oil, sprinkle on most of the parsley and season with salt and pepper. Set aside while you get the fire hot – in the fridge if it's a hot day.

Fire up your barbecue ready for direct grilling, but leaving a good space fire-free so you can cook the beurre blanc gently.

Set a small heavy-based pan over the fire and pour in the Pernod and vinegar. Add the shallot and simmer until the liquid has reduced by a just over half – you want to be left with a couple of tablespoons. Drain through a sieve into a small bowl. Rinse the pan and pour the liquid back in. Take a little bowl with a handful of ice cubes to the fire, just in case the sauce starts to split.

Add the cream and set over a low heat, so a good way from the fire. Once simmering, start to drop in the cubes of butter. Use a balloon whisk to emulsify the butter into the sauce as it melts. Don't add the butter too fast, just one cube at a time, whisking well between each addition. If the sauce looks to be going a little granular it may be splitting. In which case stop, remove the pan from the heat and drop in an ice cube, whisking hard until it melts. Then you can continue to add the butter. Once all the butter is incorporated, season to taste with salt and pepper. Slide the pan off the heat to keep warm.

Serves 2

1 live lobster, about 1.2–1.4kg (2lb 10oz–3lb 2oz)
olive oil, to drizzle
a few sprigs of flat-leaf parsley, leaves chopped
flaked sea salt and freshly ground black pepper

For the Pernod beurre blanc

6 tbsp Pernod
2 tbsp white wine vinegar
1 banana shallot, finely chopped
2 tbsp double (heavy) cream
200g (7oz) cold butter, chopped into 1cm (½in) cubes
a few ice cubes, if needed

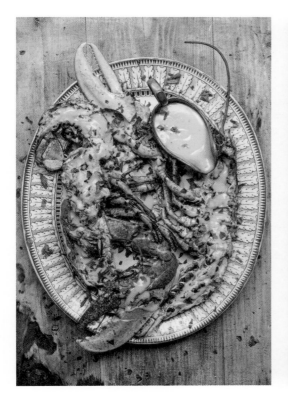

Make sure the fire is hot now, so lid off and perhaps add more fuel if necessary.

Rest the lobster cut-side down over the fire and grill over a high heat for 3 minutes or so until lightly charred. Turn and grill shell-side down for another 2–3 minutes until the flesh is cooked through. It will go opaque like a prawn when it is cooked.

To serve, rest the lobster cut-side up on a platter, drizzle over a little of the butter sauce and pour the rest into a serving bowl. Sprinkle over the reserved parsley and tuck in. Just as in the crab recipe before, select your blunt instrument and picker to get access to the claw meat. And don't forget to scoop up the shells for stock making (page 35).

Prawns and shrimps – a barbecue classic

Bung another shrimp on the barbie (Bruce?) … there is a reason prawns (or shrimp, depending where you live) fall within our top five favourites. Amazing on the grill, they cook quickly and take to smoke and different flavours so well, and frankly they taste delicious. But – there's always a but – sourcing good sustainable prawns is mighty challenging, to say the least, to the point I seriously considered leaving them out.

The large, or king, prawns we like to eat are tropical creatures and the vast majority of those are farmed in conditions not necessarily good for either the planet or the farm workers. The bad farming practices are at least being recognized and a lot of work is being done globally to improve the situation. Our best current option is to seek prawns that have an Aquaculture Stewardship Council mark or ASC (page 10) and ideally try to buy organic ones. And last but not least, just don't eat them very often; they should be a rare treat to savour, rather than a regular fixture. Small coldwater prawns are a far more sustainable choice but sadly you can only buy them ready cooked, which doesn't make them a great deal of use for your barbecue. I searched high and low to find someone, somewhere, who would sell me raw coldwater prawns but to no avail.

So, with a hint of reluctance, I give you just one prawn recipe here and another – some tasty skewers – on page 137. Enjoy them, just occasionally.

Grilled prawns with garam masala butter

I always score down the back of the shell when I grill whole unpeeled prawns; that way they open out (or 'butterfly') to reveal the meat, which means more access for the flavoured butter post-cook. It's not hard but you do need a sharp knife and a firm grip. This garlicky garam masala butter is an absolute winner, but should you fancy something else, any of the flavoured butters in the book would be great too.

Rest a prawn on a board with the back facing your dominant cutting hand. Use flat fingers on your other hand to press firmly down to tension the body and make cutting both easier and safer. Take a really sharp knife and slice through the shell a few millimetres into the flesh, then repeat with the others. Once they are all scored, use a finger to wipe out the vein running just inside the cut.

Fire up the barbecue ready for hot direct grilling.

Tip the coriander and cumin seeds, cinnamon, peppercorns, cardamon and cloves into a flameproof frying pan (one that is generous enough to fit the prawns) and set over the fire to toast for a couple of minutes. Tip the lot into a spice mill or pestle and mortar and grind to a powder.

Set the pan back over the fire and drop in the butter, allowing it to melt. Once melted, slide the pan off the heat and add the garlic and garam masala, stirring together to combine. Leave to one side to keep warm while you grill the prawns.

I always cook smaller things like prawns on a grill tray (page 24) as you can essentially stir-fry them, tossing them about a bit which is way easier than individually turning each prawn. If you don't have one, it's fine – it's just a little more of a fiddle with the tongs.

Make sure the barbecue is really hot, so take the lid off to allow for maximum oxygen flow (page 28). Spread the prawns out over the fire, either on a grill tray or directly on the grill bars, and sprinkle over the salt. Cook for a couple of minutes before turning and cooking for another minute or two – they are done when they are pink all over. Scoop up and add to the pan of spiced butter, tossing to coat. Sprinkle with coriander and chilli and serve straight away.

Serves 2–4, depending on greed

1kg (2lb 4oz) large raw shell-on prawns (shrimp)
1 tbsp flaked sea salt

For the garam masala butter

2 tbsp coriander seeds
1 tbsp cumin seeds
2cm (¾in) piece of cinnamon stick, crumbled
1 tsp black peppercorns
10 cardamon pods
5 cloves
125g (5oz) butter
2 garlic cloves, crushed

For the garnish

a little chopped coriander (cilantro)
sliced red chilli

Langoustine, tarragon and chive butter

If you can get big raw langoustine, or Dublin Bay prawns, they are a real treat grilled over hot coals. They are related to lobsters but sized like prawns and sold marked with a range of numbers – something like 9/12 or 17/25, meaning that's how many you get per pack. The smaller the number, the bigger the langoustine. The small ones are not really worth grilling, as they are pretty fiddly and the meat can dry out, so treat yourself to the big ones. The butter works well with all seafood, and it freezes like a dream so is a nice thing to find tucked away in the corner of the freezer.

Make sure you scoop up the shells and make stock (page 35); there's so much flavour potential just begging to be released.

To make the butter, add everything to a small bowl and mash together with a fork. Scoop onto a sheet of baking parchment and roll up into a slim log. The butter will happily keep in the fridge for a couple of days, well wrapped, or in the freezer for 3 months if you want to get ahead.

Fire up the barbecue ready for hot direct grilling, spreading the embers out in a thin, even layer.

While it is heating, prep the langoustine. Lay on a board and carefully, using a large sharp knife, slice in half lengthways to expose the meat. Drizzle over a little olive oil and season well with salt.

Slice the butter into rounds, allowing one slice per langoustine.

Lay the langoustine, cut-side down, over the grill for 1–2 minutes, then turn and grill shell-side down. Pile onto a warm platter and with a slice of butter each.

Serves 2

700–800g (1lb 9oz–1lb 12oz) large raw langoustine, thawed if frozen
a little olive oil
flaked sea salt

For the tarragon and chive butter

100g (3½oz) butter, slightly softened
2 garlic cloves
20g (¾oz) bunch of tarragon, leaves picked and chopped
10g (⅓oz) chives, chopped
flaked sea salt and freshly ground black pepper

Chapter 7:
Fish in a pan

This short and sweet chapter is all about taking a pan out to your fire. Fire is the original cooking tool the world over, but yes, you could definitely cook all of the following in the comfort of your own kitchen if you wanted to. My personal take is, providing it's not blowing an absolute hooley, I think there are a myriad of ways to enjoy cooking outside over and above actual barbecue grilling.

All these recipes can be cooked on a regular barbecue, or over an open wood fire either with a grill surface or the ability to hang a pot. Head back to pages 22–31 for kit and fire chat. I would probably favour an open fire here – for me, the most sociable of cooking methods, if not the most fuel efficient, where you can gather your mates, pull up a few chairs and open a bottle. With a little bit of 'boy scout' prep beforehand in the kitchen you can just hang out and chat with not much more than the occasional adding of an ingredient or a gentle stir. Blissful.

Mussel chowder

This is a perfect thing to cook with friends, gathered around an open fire, when there's just a little chill in the air. Steamy hot, comforting, and you can drink the rest of the wine you don't use in the soup. Sounds like a perfect autumn evening to me.

Clams are traditional in a chowder, but mussels are cheaper and as my number-one sustainable seafood choice I was just itching to squeeze in one more mussel recipe. If you are pescatarian, omit the bacon, but you may need to add a dash more oil for frying the base and consider a pinch or two of smoked paprika to add a little smokiness.

Light a fire – either an open fire with a grill grate or a regular barbecue – and get it ready for two-zone cooking so you can cook by direct and indirect heat (page 31).

Tip the mussels into a colander and wash and de-beard under cold running water, then drain and tip into a bowl.

Rub a little of the oil over the corn cobs and sprinkle on just a little of the oregano. Season well with salt and pepper.

Set a large saucepan (a flameproof casserole is ideal) over the indirect side of the barbecue and pour in the rest of the olive oil. Add the bacon, celery, onions, carrots, bay leaves and the rest of the oregano. Set a lid loosely over the pan, or cover with foil, and sweat gently for a good 30–40 minutes until everything is super-soft and very lightly caramelized. I think this is a step to take your time with. You will be rewarded with flavour, so don't rush.

Meanwhile, set a grill tray over the direct fire and tip on the mussels. Cover the tray loosely with foil and allow them to steam open. Remove and leave to cool a little, then pick two-thirds of the mussels from their shells, leaving the rest in the shells. Reserve.

Serves 4–6

1kg (2lb 4oz) mussels
3 tbsp olive oil
2 corn on the cob
2 tsp dried oregano
200g (7oz) smoked streaky bacon, snipped into 1cm (½in) pieces
3 celery stalks
2 onions, finely chopped
2 carrots, finely chopped
3 bay leaves
250ml (9fl oz/1 cup) white wine
1 tbsp plain (all-purpose) flour
700g (1lb 9oz) potatoes, peeled and cut into 3cm (1¼in) cubes
750ml (25fl oz/3 cups) fish stock
200ml (7fl oz/scant 1 cup) double (heavy) cream
a good handful of flat-leaf parsley, about 15g (½oz)
flaked sea salt and freshly ground black pepper

To serve
Tabasco or other hot sauce

Set the corn cobs over the fire and cook until lightly charred, turning regularly, then remove and allow to cool a little. Rest vertically on a board and use a sharp knife to shim off the kernels. Scoop into a bowl and take to the fire along with the wine, flour, potatoes and stock.

Once the veg are all soft, pour in the wine and slide the pan over a high heat to allow it to bubble and reduce. Once the liquid has nearly all gone, sprinkle over the flour and stir to mix. Add the potatoes, corn kernels and stock and season well with salt and pepper, stirring well. Slide the pan a little further from the heat, loosely cover again and leave to bubble away until the potatoes are soft and tender but not collapsing, maybe another 30 minutes or so, adding a splash of water if it's getting a little dry. Finally stir through the cream, the picked mussel meat and the shelled mussels and most of the parsley and heat through for a few minutes.

Spoon into warmed bowls, or serve in a large tureen if you're feeling a little fancy, scattered with the rest of the parsley. Tuck in while steaming hot, perhaps with a shake of hot sauce, if you like.

Monkfish and chard paella

Paella is traditionally cooked over an open wood fire and this is the way I like to do it, although you can also set the pan over a charcoal barbecue, maybe adding a little smoking wood if you have some. As with all the recipes in this chapter, the hob in your kitchen would work too. The golden rule with any paella? Do not stir the pan. The goal here is to develop a sticky light charred crust that you scrape off when serving. Called the socarrat, it's the highly prized best bit, so no stirring!

First light your fire – either an open wood fire, or a charcoal barbecue with a little added wood if you like. If you are using good fuel (page 12), you can start to cook as soon as the fire has a little heat; there's no need at all to wait until it is burnt to embers as you are simply wasting heat energy.

Set a flameproof paella or deep frying pan over the fire and tip in the fennel seeds, toasting for a few minutes. Scoop into a pestle and mortar and grind to a powder. Set aside.

Pour the olive oil into the pan and add the onions, cooking gently over a low heat until softening and lightly caramelized, a good 20–30 minutes. At the same time, pour the stock into a flameproof saucepan and sprinkle in the saffron, setting the pan over the fire to heat up.

Add the tomatoes, garlic and ground fennel to the pan of onions and stir for a minute or two before pouring in the sherry, allowing it to bubble and evaporate. Stir through the rice and pour over the hot saffron-infused stock. Season with salt and pepper and stir, then cover the pan with foil. Leave to cook for about 20 minutes until the rice is not quite tender. Don't stir the pan – the sticky burnt on bits are prized!

While the rice is cooking, drizzle a little olive oil over the chard stems and leaves. Rest them over the fire to grill for a few minutes until tender – the stems will take longer – then remove and chop into bite-sized pieces.

Lift the foil and scatter over the monkfish and grilled chard, pushing it into the rice but still without stirring. Re-cover with the foil and cook for another 10 minutes or so until the fish is cooked through. Lightly fold through the fish and chard, then scatter with a little parsley and a good drizzle of extra virgin olive oil. Serve with lemon wedges to squeeze over.

Serves 4–6

1 tbsp fennel seeds
2 tbsp olive oil, plus extra to drizzle
2 large red onions, finely chopped
900ml (32fl oz/3¾cups) fish stock (you could use either light, rich or seafood stock for this, pages 33–35)
a big pinch of saffron threads, about ½ tsp
200g (7oz) cherry tomatoes, quartered
3 garlic cloves, crushed to a paste
150ml (5fl oz/scant ⅔ cup) dry sherry, fino, manzanilla or dry oloroso – all great
300g (10½oz) paella rice
350g (12oz) chard, stems separated from leaves
500g (1lb 2oz) monkfish, cut into 2–3cm (¾–1¼in) pieces
flaked sea salt and freshly ground black pepper

To serve

chopped flat-leaf parsley
extra virgin olive oil
lemon wedges

Black rice with grilled cuttlefish and aioli

Black rice, or arroz negro, is a paella-style dish where a little cuttle or squid ink is used to dramatic effect. It looks fab and tastes delicious and is often served with seafood. The kiwi may feel a little weird in the marinade, and it is certainly not traditional, but it contains a plentiful amount of an enzymatic compound that's really effective at tenderizing proteins. A little mashed kiwi is one of the best things I know for tenderizing cuttle or squid, keeping it soft and tender, and you don't taste it when it's cooked. Unless you are lucky enough to find an un-pierced ink sac when you are prepping (page 199), your fishmonger is the best place to buy the ink. They should have sachets of it tucked away on a shelf.

Light a fire ready for direct and indirect cooking, either an open fire with a grill surface or a regular barbecue.

Slice the cuttlefish into bite-sized strips of about 1cm (½in) thick and drop into a bowl along with the tentacles. Peel the kiwi and finely chop, mashing with the flat of your knife to give you a coarse purée. Scoop onto the cuttlefish with a couple of tablespoons of the olive oil and a generous grind of salt and pepper. Stir well and slide into the fridge to marinate for 30 minutes.

Pour the rest of the oil into a large, heavy-based frying pan (if you have a paella pan, all the better) and set over a medium heat on the fire. Add the onions and leave to soften and colour lightly for a good 20 minutes, stirring a few times. Slide the pan a little further from the fire if they are colouring too quickly.

While the onion is softening, make the aioli. Pound the garlic with the salt in a pestle and mortar until you have a creamy paste. Add the egg yolks and mix together really thoroughly. Start by adding the oils drop by drop, mixing really well between each addition. Once it starts to thicken and emulsify you can increase the rate of oil you add to a little trickle but take care not to go too fast. If it gets too thick to stir, add a squeeze of lemon juice to thin it a little. Once you have added all the oil, season with the lemon juice and plenty of pepper. You can also make this in a bowl with a balloon whisk or in a food processor, adding the oil little by little down the spout with the motor running.

Serves 4–6

1kg (2lb 4oz) cuttlefish, cleaned and prepped (page 199)
2 kiwi fruit
4 tbsp olive oil
2 onions, chopped
5 large vine tomatoes, finely chopped
3 garlic cloves, finely chopped
2 tsp smoked paprika
150ml (5fl oz/scant ⅔ cup) white wine
300g (10½oz) paella rice
3–4 x 4g sachets of cuttle or squid ink
900g fish stock (page 35)
a few sprigs of flat-leaf parsley, chopped
flaked sea salt and freshly ground black pepper

Back at the fire, slide the pan over a slightly higher heat and add the tomatoes, along with the garlic, smoked paprika and a good seasoning of salt and pepper. Cook for another 10 minutes until the tomatoes have collapsed, then pour in the wine, stirring well to mix, and simmer until reduced to a fairly thick sauce.

Stir through the rice and squid ink thoroughly, then pour in the stock, giving it a good stir to mix. Cover the pan loosely with foil and leave to cook for around 20 minutes without stirring.

While the rice is cooking, thread the cuttlefish over 4–6 metal skewers and set aside on a plate.

Once the rice is done, remove from the fire and leave to rest, still covered, while you cook the cuttlefish. Rest the skewers over a really high direct heat for just a couple of minutes until lightly charred and opaque.

Remove the foil from the rice and fluff up the grains a little with a fork. Rest the skewers on top and scatter over the parsley. Serve straight away with the aioli on the side.

For the aioli

4 fat garlic cloves
1 tsp flaked sea salt
2 egg yolks
150ml (5fl oz/scant ⅔ cup) extra
    virgin olive oil
150ml (5fl oz/⅔ cup) neutral
    oil such as sunflower or
    vegetable
juice of 1 lemon
freshly ground black pepper

You also need 4–6 metal skewers

Sri Lankan crab curry

Crab curry is found all over the place in Sri Lanka, one of the most beautiful countries I've been lucky enough to visit. Yes, eating this is a big messy old job but it's a fun and very tasty thing to share with friends. If the crab is off-putting – my kids won't eat it, I get it – make the curry base and drop in around 1kg (2lb 4oz) of cubed fish to simmer for the last 10 minutes or so. Anything that holds together well will do just fine.

The coconut sprinkles make this dish for me – they are addictive. Sadly not my idea but nicked (with permission!) from the lovely chef Karan Gokani whose book *Hoppers* is a Sri Lankan food delight.

Also, an apology for two pretty difficult ingredients to source – both pandan leaves (or screwpine) and goraka are not to be found in a supermarket. Goraka brings a little sourness to the party; the nearest equivalent is tamarind so you could use that if pushed, but there is really no alternative to pandan leaves other than to leave them out and use more curry leaves. As is usual for anything tricky, online is the best place to find them.

I tend to make the curry powder on the hob for convenience, as it's a job you can do a few days in advance of cooking. Set a small frying pan over a medium heat and toast the spices and rice one variety at a time until they are golden and smelling delicious. Tip each onto a big plate as you go, allowing everything to cool. Put the curry leaves into the pan and toast until dry, then leave to cool on the plate. Repeat with the pandan leaves. Once everything is cool, use a spice grinder to blitz to a powder. Tip into a airtight container – a jam jar is a good thing here – and set aside until you are ready to cook.

Freeze and mechanically kill the crab (page 233).

Once you have dispatched the crab, you can remove the legs from the body. With a good grip they should twist off fairly easily. Remove and discard the frilly gills and the small gut sac in the centre of the carapace, then scoop out any brown meat and set aside in a bowl. Reserve the shell for making stock (page 37).

When you are ready to cook, light a fire ready for direct and indirect cooking – either an open fire with a grill surface, or a regular barbecue.

Serves 4–6

For the curry powder
2 tbsp coriander seeds
1 tbsp cumin seeds
2 tsp black peppercorns
2 tsp fennel seeds
1 tsp fenugreek seeds
1 tsp cardamon pods
½ tsp cloves
1 tbsp basmati rice
a few sprigs of fresh curry leaves, about 10g (⅓oz)
a few pandan leaves, snipped into 2cm (¾in) lengths

For the curry
2 tbsp vegetable oil
4–6 hot green chillies, halved lengthways (or to taste)
2 red onions, finely chopped
4 fat garlic cloves, crushed to a paste

Set a large casserole pot slightly off the side of the fire to give a low–medium heat. Pour in the oil and add the green chillies, onions, garlic and cinnamon stick. Bruise the lemongrass stalks with the flat of a large knife and drop into the pot. Give everything a good stir and leave to fry gently for a good 15–20 minutes until the onion is soft and lightly coloured.

Make the coconut sprinkles at the same time. Set a small frying pan over the fire and pour in the oil. Add the bruised fennel and cumin seeds and fry for just 30 seconds before adding the onion. Fry for 10 minutes until the onion is softening, then add the garlic and stir for another minute. Tip in the coconut and add the curry leaves, chilli flakes and turmeric. Season well with salt and pepper and fry for a few minutes until the coconut is a deep golden brown. Scoop into a serving bowl and set aside.

Add the curry powder, the goraka and pandan to the casserole pot and stir for a few minutes. Pour in the stock and coconut milk and bring up to the boil, then simmer steadily for around 15 minutes until slightly thickened.

Spread the prepared crab legs out over the grill bars and grill over a high heat for 10 minutes. Then drop into the sauce, along with any brown meat, and stir together, just trying to submerge it as best you can. Loosely cover the pot and simmer for another 5 minutes, stirring a couple of times.

Transfer to a large serving dish, or serve straight from the pan, sprinkled with a little coconut mix, serving the rest alongside. Eat with plenty of warmed naan bread, allowing people to help themselves to crab and sauce – finger bowls and napkins at the ready.

Head on back to page 233 for my thoughts on how to tackle a crab leg. And consider scooping up all the shells after you've eaten to make the most excellent curry-tinged stock, freezing them to do another time if you'd rather (page 17).

1 cinnamon stick, snapped into 2cm (¾in) pieces
2 lemongrass stalks, halved lengthways
3 pieces of goraka
5cm (2in) pandan leaf
½ tsp ground turmeric
600ml (20fl oz/2½ cups) fish stock
400ml (13fl oz/generous 1½ cups) can of coconut milk
about 3kg (7lb) live crab, spider or brown

For the coconut sprinkles

2 tbsp vegetable oil
1 tsp fennel seeds, bruised in a pestle and mortar
1 tsp cumin seeds, bruised in a pestle and mortar
1 red onion, finely chopped
4 garlic cloves, finely chopped
100g (3½oz/heaped 1 cup) desiccated (dried shredded) coconut
5g (⅛oz) fresh curry leaves
1–2 tsp dried chilli (hot pepper) flakes
½ tsp ground turmeric
flaked sea salt and freshly ground black pepper

To serve

warmed naan

Serrano ham grilled hake with Spanish bean stew

The ham protects the delicate fish fillets from the heat of the fire and does a great job of preventing sticking. Skinned white fish fillets are not easy things to grill on their own because of their low fat content, so if you are a pescatarian you would be better off grilling oily fish fillets, like mackerel, and serving them with the stew.

Fire up the barbecue ready for direct and indirect grilling so you can slide the stew between the two sides to control the cooking temperature. You can also cook the stew on the hob inside if you are short of grill space.

Pour the olive oil in a large, heavy-based saucepan and add the onions, celery, peppers and bay leaves. Fry gently over a low heat until soft and lightly browned and then add the garlic and tomatoes. Stir for a few minutes until the tomatoes are collapsing, then pour in the sherry and let it reduce for a few minutes. Add the cannellini and butter beans, smoked paprika and the saffron and soaking water, stirring over the heat for another couple of minutes.

Add the stock and half the parsley and season well with salt and pepper, then simmer for around 10–15 minutes until the sauce has thickened. Slide off the heat to the indirect side of the barbecue and set a grill tray over the fire to heat up ready for cooking the fish. You can also cook direct on hot, clean grill bars here too, as the ham will offer some protection from sticking.

Lay the hake fillets on a chopping board and wrap each one in a couple of slices of Serrano ham to enclose it as much as possible. Drizzle a little oil all over and season lightly with salt and pepper.

Rest the parcels on the grill tray and cook for about 10–12 minutes, turning once or twice, until the ham is lightly crisp and the fish is 60°C (140°F) when probed in the centre.

To serve, spoon the stew into bowls and top with the hake. Sprinkle over the rest of the parsley and a good drizzle of extra virgin olive oil.

Serves 4

4 x 125g (5oz) hake fillets
8 slices of Serrano ham
a drizzle of olive oil
flaked sea salt and freshly ground
    black pepper

For the stew

4 tbsp olive oil
2 onions, chopped
2 celery stalks, chopped
2 red (bell) peppers, chopped
2 bay leaves
3 garlic cloves, finely sliced
5 medium tomatoes, chopped
3 tbsp dry sherry (or dry white
    wine)
400g (14oz) can of cannellini
    beans, drained and rinsed
400g (14oz) can of butter (lima)
    beans, drained and rinsed
1 tsp smoked paprika
a large pinch of saffron soaked
    in 1 tbsp boiling water for
    10 minutes
350ml (12¼fl oz/1½ cups) fish
    stock
a good handful of flat-leaf
    parsley, chopped
extra virgin olive oil, to drizzle

Cambodian-style fish curry

Cambodia is another extraordinarily lovely country with a rich tradition of cooking fish over fire. I still dream of the food we ate on a trip there years ago; I'd go back in a heartbeat. The national dish is 'fish amok', where fish is steamed in a banana leaf boat in an awesome coconut curry sauce. I tried hard to replicate it at home but the truth is, folding leaves into boats is way beyond my origami skill level. So here I give you all the flavours I remember in a far easier cooked-in-a-pan form. The dish begins by making the kroeung, or curry paste.

If you are cooking outside, light your barbecue or fire pit ready for direct cooking but, as always, leave a fire-free zone for heat control.

Begin with the kroeung, or spice paste, by adding the tomatoes, shallots, turmeric, shrimp paste, garlic, lemongrass, lime leaves and chilli flakes to a small food processor. Add the vegetable oil and 3 tablespoons of water and blitz to a paste.

Set a large, deep frying pan over the heat and add the kroeung. Cook over a fairly gentle heat, stirring frequently, for about 15 minutes to simmer out the water and fry the paste until thickened.

Pour in the coconut milk, add the lime juice and brown sugar and season with salt and pepper. Simmer for a further 10 minutes, stirring a couple of times.

Meanwhile, if you are cooking outside you can grill the beans to give them an extra layer of flavour. Simply drizzle the oil over them and season with a little salt and pepper. Grill over a direct heat for just 3–4 minutes. If you have a grill tray it's a good time to use it to make sure you lose none to the fire, although you can cook them perpendicular to the grill bars and turn gently. Once cooked, transfer to a board and chop into bite-sized pieces and set aside. If you are cooking on the hob, blanch in boiling water for 3–4 minutes before draining and setting aside.

Drop the fish cubes into the curry sauce, turning gently to mix, then scatter the beans over the top. Cover the pan with a lid or piece of foil and simmer for 5 minutes to cook the fish and heat the beans through.

Serve scattered with coriander and a little chopped bird's-eye chilli for extra punch.

Serves 4

For the kroeung

100g (3½oz) cherry tomatoes, halved

2 banana shallots, roughly chopped

50g (2oz) turmeric root or 1 tbsp ground turmeric

10g (⅓oz) shrimp paste (or fish sauce)

4 garlic cloves

2 fat lemongrass stalks, roughly chopped

2 double-lobed lime leaves

1–2 tsp dried chilli (hot pepper) flakes, to taste

2 tbsp vegetable oil

For the curry

400ml (13fl oz/generous 1½ cups) coconut milk

juice of 1 lime

1–2 tsp palm or brown sugar, to taste

1 tbsp vegetable oil

300g (10½oz) stringless runner beans, topped and tailed

800g (1lb 12oz) white fish fillets, cut into 3cm (1¼in) cubes

flaked sea salt and freshly ground black pepper

a little coriander (cilantro) and fresh chopped bird's-eye chilli, to garnish

Index

INFORMATION

Exploring good fish choices

Marine Stewardship Council
Globally
https://www.msc.org/

UK
https://www.msc.org/uk
Sustainability: https://www.msc.org/
what-you-can-do/eat-sustainable-
seafood/fish-to-eat

In the UK
Marine Conservation Society
https://www.mcsuk.org/goodfishguide

Cornwall Good Seafood Guide
www.cornwallgoodseafoodguide.org.uk

Fishing into the Future
Aimed at fishing professionals, but useful
for a deep dive into the issues
https://www.fishingintothefuture.co.uk/
https://www.fishingporthole.co.uk/

Discover Seafood
UK seasonality lists
https://discoverseafood.uk/seafood/

In the USA
Seafood Watch
https://www.seafoodwatch.org/

In Australia
Good Fish
https://goodfish.org.au/

SUPPLIERS

**Here are the places I bought seafood
during the writing of this book**

In person:
Bristol Fish
https://bristolfish.com/

The Chelsea Fishmonger, Rex Goldsmith
http://www.thechelseafishmonger.co.uk/

The Fish Shop, Bristol
https://lovethefishshop.co.uk/

Online:
The Cornish Fishmonger – Cornish fish
specialists
https://thecornishfishmonger.co.uk/

Pesky fish – online fish market, impeccable
sourcing
https://peskyfish.co.uk

Chalk Stream Trout – large trout
specialists
http://www.chalkstreamfoods.co.uk/

Mere Trout – smaller trout
https://www.meretrout.com/

W Harvey and Sons – shellfish specialists
https://crabmeat.co.uk/

Cornish Seaweed – wild harvested
seaweeds
https://www.cornishseaweed.co.uk/

Suppliers from my Instagram followers

Here follows a long list of names from my Instagram followers (thank you!), not exhaustive by any means but a little way for me to shout out all the good fishmongers out there! Many below sell online and deliver nationally, while some you will just need to turn up in person. I don't have space to give contact details but, as ever, the internet is your friend!

Scotland

Amity Fish, Peterhead
Blue Flag Seafoods, Aberdeen
D R Collin, Eyemouth
D Watts and Sons, Oban
David Lowrie Fish
Eat Mair Fish, Buckie
Fishbox UK, Peterhead
Granite City Fish, Aberdeen
Inshore fish supply, Macduff
Keltic Seafare, Dingwall
Pieroni's Fish, Ayr
Pittenweem Fish House, Anstruther
Pro Fish, Aviemore
The Fish People, Glasgow
Welch Fishmongers, Edinburgh

Wales

Ashton Fishmongers, Cardiff Indoor Market
Cardigan Bay Fish, St Dodmaels
Catch of the Day, Aberteifi
Coakleys, Mumbles
Lockdown Lobsters, North Wales
Mermaid Seafoods, Llandudno
Selwyn's Seafoods, Swansea
Swansea Fish, Swansea
Tuckers, Swansea

Ireland and Northern Ireland

Ballycotton Seafood, Cork
Donegal Prime Fish, Derry
Ewing's Seafood, Belfast
Foyle Bia Mara, Donegal
Keenans Seafood, Belfast
Moore on the Quay, Foyle Marina
Sea Source, Newry
Something Fishy NI Ltd, Portavogie
St George's Market, Belfast
The Catch Fish Shop, Dublin
Walter Ewing, Belfast

Northern England

Alfred Enderby, Grimsby
Bolton Market, Bolton
Bricklands Fish and Seafood, Chester
Cheshire Fish, Macclesfield
Chester Market Fishmongers, Chester
Cod and Lobster, Scarborough
Collingwood seafood, North Shields
Direct Fisheries, Manchester
EasyFish Co, Heaton Moor
Fleetwood Wellgate Fisheries, Clitheroe
Fowlers Of York, York
Hodgson Fish, Hartlepool
Kermelly's, Isle of Man
Kirkgate Market, Leeds
Ocean Wave Fresh Fish, Cheshire
Out of the Blue Fishmongers, Manchester
Premier Seafoods, Grimsby
Tarbett's, Leeds, Harrogate
The Fairy Cod Mother, Darwen Market

Eastern England

A Passion for Seafood, Woodbridge
Crystal Waters, Saffron Walden
Deliver Fish Ltd, Lowestoft
Fresh Fish, Rushden
Hobbs Fishmongers, Market Harborough
James Hunt Fisheries, Felixstowe
Osborne's, Leigh on Sea
The Cambridge Fishmonger, Cambridge
Valkyrie Fresh Catch, Colchester
World of Fish, Lowestoft
Young's Fish Ltd, Chelmsford

Southern England

Aldens Fish Market, Oxford
Arcade Fisheries, Hastings
Bembridge Fish, Isle of Wight
Bethnal Green Fishmongers, London
Bickerstaffs, Newhaven
Bradleys Fish, Southampton
Brighton and Newhaven Fish Sales, Brighton
Browns Seafood, Littlehampton
Cranleigh Fish, Cranleigh
Dungeness Fish Hut, Dungeness
Ellis and Jones, Greenwich
Fin and Flounder, London
Fish Glorious Fish, Casey Fields Farm Shop, Berkshire
Furness Fish Markets, London
GCH Fishmongers, Bedford
Hampstead Fishmonger, London

Henderson to Home
Hollowshore Fisheries, Faversham
Hutchings Brothers Seafood,
    Bournemouth
Jonathan Norris Fishmonger,
    London
Johnsons Fish, Portsmouth
JS Fresh Fish, Southampton
Life of Fish, London
London Shell Co., London
Moxons Fresh Fish, London
New Forest Fish and Shellfish,
    Hampshire
New Wave Seafood, Cirencester
Notting Hill Fish Shop, London
Oeno Maris, London
Padstow Fish, Cheltenham
Pearl Fisheries, Beckenham
Premier Fish at Home, Salisbury
Pure Seafood, Sussex
Rock A Nore Fisheries, Hastings
Rockfish UK
Rye Bay Fish, Rye
Sandys Fishmongers,
    Twickenham
Sankeys Fishmongers, Tunbridge
    Wells and Tonbridge
Simply Oysters
Simply Seafoods, Solihull
Something Fishy, Chichester
Southern Head Fishing, Eastborne
Steve Hatt Fishmongers, London
The Fish Shop, Camberley
The Fish Society, Guildford
The Fishmongers Kitchen,
    London

The Fresh Fish Shop, Haywards
    Heath
The Goods Shed, Canterbury
The Highbury Fishmongers,
    London
The Musselman, Surrey
The Upper Scale, London
The Sea, The Sea, London
The Wild Fish Project, Guildford
Veasey & Sons, Forest Row
Williams and Bunkell, Claygate
Wright Brothers, London

Western England
AB Seafoods, Paignton
Beer Fisheries, Seaton
Bodmin Seafoods, Bodmin
Catch of the Day, Kingsbridge
Conscious Food Co., Bristol
Clifton Seafood Co., Bristol
Curgurrell Farm Shop, Portscatho
Devon and Cornwall Fish,
    Appledore
Devon Quality Fish, Exmouth
Davy's Locker, Bridport
Dorset Shellfish, Portland
Fish for Thought, Bodmin
Flying Fish Seafoods, Saint
    Columb
Frazers Scallops, Brixham
Fresco Fishmarket, Bristol
Fresh Cornish Fish, Penzance
George Cleave Fish Merchant,
    Wadebridge
Greendale Seafood, Sidmouth

Greenslade Fish, Poole
Hamiltons Fish, Torquay
Kernow Catch, St Agnes
Kernow Fisheries, Falmouth
Kernow Sashimi, Helston
Lyme Bay Fish Shack, Axminster
Mark Lobb, Dartmouth
Net and Line, Bath
Off the Hook Fishmongers,
    Wadebridge
Parkstone Fisheries, Poole
Pysk Fish, Falmouth
R G Seafoods, Torpoint
Smithfish, Bristol
Sound Seafood, Plymouth
Sole of Discretion, Plymouth
Stream Farm, Bridgewater
The Devon Fishmonger, Honiton
Weyfish, Weymouth
White Row Farm, Frome

ACKNOWLEDGEMENTS

ACKNOWLEDGEMENTS

Writing a book is a solitary activity but, much as I love that, it takes an army to accomplish the end result. Many people have been involved in the making of SCORCHED and I want to try and thank them.

The photography part of a creating a cookbook is huge, the moment the whole thing starts to come alive, out of my head, off the page. The beautiful pictures you see here are the product of many days' hard graft, often in tough weather, oscillating from storms to heatwaves, and I hope they make my food look both irresistible and achievable. Huge thanks to Jason, brilliant photographer and longtime collaborator who somehow always works miracles (do any of these pictures look like they were taken in a gale?!). Big love to Becky, shoot assistant, my right hand woman at Bristol Fire School, and a constant support during the writing of this book. I appreciate it all. Jaine Bevan, for sourcing so many gorgeous props to compliment my raggle-taggle collection of homemade plates and bowls. Extra hands on shoot days are a godsend. Thanks to Gordon @HalifaxSmokeBox (who also built my cold smoker), Amanda @SageandSeason, and Ben @BenNeale29, thanks for rolling up your sleeves!

I am lucky to count some of the best in the UK fire-world as friends. Matt of Whittle and Flame, thanks for making the best charcoal I ever burnt, and for being generally gert lush. Chief Kweef, another totally lushy one, I just love our fishy cooks fuelled by wine and giggles. Olly at Meatmatters, thanks for listening to my occasional rants about life down the wire. My band of merry Fire Pirates, Si, Joe, Dan, Henry – let's spark up soon, I miss cooking and playing with you – and my fellow pyromaniacs, Andy, Elliot, Chris, Christian, thanks for the excess of good times.

On a more sensible note, I spoke and hung out with many people way more experienced in fish and fishing than I will ever be. Firstly 'Sam the Fish', of Bristol Fish, who went above and beyond his fishmonger duties to get me all the fish for the shoots, which irritatingly always seemed to fall on his day off. Big thanks to Mike Warner from A Passion for Seafood, and Emma Plotnek of Fishing into the Future, for your help in navigating a somewhat tricky line around just what responsible fish eating should look like. Rex, aka The Chelsea Fishmonger, thanks for letting me come and work the other side of the fish counter those chilly couple of day. So inspiring to see your team excelling at their craft. Simon Stallard, thanks for your incredible hospitality and knowledge and for driving me around Cornwall in search of good fish.

To my YETI family – in the UK, Nick, Lauren and Rowan; in the US, Doc, LeighAnn and Andrew, I'm looking forward to lots more fun in the wild. Thanks for the BEST kit ever. And my Weber family: you know I couldn't live without my iconic kettle BBQs, and special thanks to Grill Masters Dan and Jon for taking me bass fishing.

Martine at Sauce Management, thanks for always being at the end of the line, and for occasionally pushing me out my comfort zone. To all at Team Quadrille, my publisher for years now, thank you for trusting me to just get on with it, and for all the attention to detail that goes on behind the scenes. Special thanks to Sofie for editorial, Alicia for the design, and Ellie for the amazing cover.

Lastly, my flesh and blood fam, whom I always seem to thank last but really they are top of the top, keeping my wheels turning in many unseen ways. My husband Rob who has never, ever tried to tame me and always has my back and my kids Izaac and Eve, who quite simply rock. I love you.

Managing Director Sarah Lavelle
Commissioning Editor Stacey Cleworth
Project Editor Sofie Shearman
Copy Editor Wendy Hobson
Designer Alicia House
Cover Illustration Ellie Foreman-Peck
Photographer Jason Ingram
Food Styling Genevieve Taylor
Prop Styling Jaine Bevan
Head of Production Stephen Lang
Production Controller Martina Georgieva

First published in 2024 by Quadrille,
an imprint of Hardie Grant Publishing

Quadrille
52–54 Southwark Street
London SE1 1UN
quadrille.com

Cataloguing in Publication Data: a catalogue record for this
book is available from the British Library.

ISBN: 978 1 83783 035 0

Printed in China